INSPECTING
A HOUSE

INSPECTING A HOUSE

A GUIDE FOR BUYERS, OWNERS, AND RENOVATORS

Third Edition

CARSON DUNLOP & ASSOCIATES LTD.

Dearborn™
Trade Publishing
A **Kaplan Professional** Company

This publication is designed to provide accurate and authoritative information in regard to the subject matter covered. It is sold with the understanding that the publisher is not engaged in rendering legal, accounting, or other professional service. If legal advice or other expert assistance is required, the services of a competent professional person should be sought.

Vice President and Publisher: Cynthia A. Zigmund
Acquisitions Editor: Mary B. Good and Laurie McGuire
Senior Managing Editor: Jack Kiburz
Interior Design: Lucy Jenkins
Cover Design: Design Solutions
Typesetting: Elizabeth Pitts

Published by Dearborn Trade Publishing
A Kaplan Professional Company

Printed in the United States of America

04 05 06 10 9 8 7 6 5 4 3 2 1

Library of Congress Cataloging-in-Publication Data

Carson, Alan.
  Inspecting a house : a guide for buyers, owners, and renovators / Carson Dunlop & Associates Ltd.—3rd ed.
      p. cm.
Includes index.
  ISBN 0-7931-8054-6 (6 × 9 paperback)
  1. Dwellings—Inspection—Handbooks, manuals, etc. 2. House buying—Handbooks, manuals, etc. 3. Dwellings—Remodeling—Handbooks, manuals, etc. I. Dunlop, Robert. II. Title.
  TH4817 .5 .C37 2004
  643′.12—dc22

                                                                    2003020325

This book is dedicated to our parents.

C o n t e n t s

SOME GENERAL ADVICE ON HOME INSPECTIONS

A house is the largest single purchase most of us will ever make. It is not only an investment, but for about 12 hours every day it is also our environment. Why is it then that so many people spend less than 45 minutes looking at the home they intend to buy? Most people have their mechanic check out a used automobile before they will spend $2,500 on it. Doesn't it make sense to check out a house worth many times that? We think it does.

While most sellers will not intentionally mislead someone, neither will they point out problems unless they are asked specifically to do so. Finding out after you move in that things are not as you thought can be frustrating and expensive. As home inspectors, we have seen new bathrooms with no piping to any of the fixtures, new electrical outlets with no wires, and great-looking furnaces that don't heat.

A basic knowledge of how houses work—and what it means when they don't—will help make you a better homebuyer. In this book, we will concentrate on the fundamentals of the home rather than on the cosmetics. Architectural styles and decorating features are matters of personal preference, and everyone is equally well qualified to judge what is right for him or her. However, most people do not have the ability to ensure that their new home will be structurally sound and keep them safe, warm, and dry. Things such as a safe, adequately sized electrical system and reliable plumbing are often taken for granted by people who lack the knowledge to evaluate them. This book is designed to give you that knowledge.

If a home inspection company is going to do the evaluation, try to be present while it is being performed. You can then ask pertinent questions and have any defects pointed out, so that you will have a better understanding of the problems.

The inspection can be conducted prior to putting in an offer, or after your offer to purchase has been accepted, if there is a clause in it that states it is conditional on a satisfactory inspection. The condition should be worded in such a way that the final decision rests with you and not the home inspection company. In fairness to the seller, the condition in the offer should have a time limitation so that the inspection is carried out promptly. Some homesellers have an inspection performed before the house is listed for sale. This gives prospective buyers a chance to learn about the condition of the house before they make an offer to buy it.

If you are performing the inspection yourself, read Chapters 1 through 9 in this book in advance. Then on the day you inspect the house, use the checklists at the end of each chapter to help you make a note of strengths and weaknesses. You will see that we suggest beginning your inspection with the outside of the property. In addition to the information you will gain about the exterior components of the house, such as roofing, brickwork, etc., you will pick up some clues about what is happening inside the house. From the outside, you can determine the location of the electrical panel in the basement by noting where the wires outside pass through the wall. You will know if the house is heated with oil from the fill lines; you will know that there is at least some galvanized piping in the house if the outside faucets are galvanized. From the outside, you can also spot some problems or symptoms: land sloping towards a house will increase the chances of the house having a wet basement, as will poor roof drainage, while exterior cracks will indicate the possibility of interior damage or movement. (For this reason, the location of any exterior cracks should be noted and the interior checked for corresponding damage.)

Inside the house, it is best to start in the basement if there is one, for this is where the nuts and bolts of the house are. On your way down to the basement, it is a good idea to turn up the thermostat a few degrees. That way you will be able to see the furnace while it is operating. The unfinished basement is where you will see the visible components of the structure: the foundation walls, beams, and joists. You will usually find the furnace, ductwork, electrical panel, exposed wiring, water heater, and piping here.

Just as you will pick up things on the outside of the house to follow up in the basement, you will find things in the basement that will give you clues about what to look for in the rest of the house. Structural defects noted outdoors or in the basement have to be followed up through the house. Termination points of all the systems should be checked. Each room should have a functional heating supply, adequate electrical outlets, and doors and windows that open and close properly. Plumbing fixtures should be operable and fireplaces should be checked. There should be adequate closet and storage space, and the house layout should work well.

The location of the attic access hatch should be found. Depending on the roof configuration, some houses have more than one attic and others have none. You should at least poke your head into the attic to look for roof leaks, condensation, insulation, ventilation, pests, and the visible structural components.

While the condition of a house is an important part of buying a home, it is only one part. Remember to keep things in perspective. A house that needs $20,000 worth of improvements may be a great investment if it is priced $30,000 below market value.

Once you find a house that fits all of your criteria, arrange an appointment to inspect it. Let the real estate agent and seller know that you will be in the house one-and-a-half to two-and-a-half hours. You will need to take some equipment on the inspection. A pair of binoculars will help you look at the roof and chimney. To check for rotten or termite-infested wood, bring a sharp probe. A measuring tape will help determine joist sizes and spans. Where the plumbing is painted, a magnet can help identify galvanized piping. An electrical tester will be useful in evaluating the wiring. If you are going to open the electrical panel, bring several screwdrivers. You may need a stepladder to get into the attic, and a strong-beam flashlight, of course, once you get up there. There is very little doubt that you will get dirty, so be sure to wear old clothes.

Try to put your emotions aside and be objective while performing the inspection. Admiring the fireplace mantle is fun, but distracting. If the seller is in the house, do not point out the flaws to him. No one appreciates being told his house is not fit to live in. If you plan to change the house, do not discuss your plans while the seller is in the room. More than one sale has been aborted because the seller didn't want to sell to someone who was going to "ruin" his home.

As you go through the house, concentrate on the major areas: the structure, roofing, plumbing, heating, wiring, windows, kitchens, and bathrooms. Do not attempt to make notes of every minor flaw. No home will be perfect, and it is important not to lose sight of the forest for the trees.

At the conclusion of the inspection, it is usually helpful to take one last walk through the house, ensuring that all the pieces of the puzzle have been put together. By reviewing the information you have collected, a clear picture of the condition of the house should develop. Adding this to the other homebuying parameters should put you in a position to make an educated buying decision. Remember, there is no such thing as too much information. One more thing: Did you turn down the thermostat?

HOME INSPECTIONS

1

THE EXTERIOR

The exterior of a house provides a first, and often lasting, impression of a property. Unfortunately, many buyers spend only enough time looking at the outside to develop that general impression. The exterior not only reveals a good deal about the overall quality of construction and maintenance, but also provides clues to problems that may be found on the inside. Consequently, an inspection should always begin on the outside and end with one last walk around the exterior.

Your inspection should start even before the house is in view. The neighborhood should be evaluated for pluses such as schools, shopping, transportation, recreational facilities, and overall landscaping. Minuses such as nearby factories, railroad tracks, heavy traffic routes, and vacant lots should also be considered. It is a good idea to find out whether there are plans for undeveloped land, for these could change the character of the neighborhood. Should resale potential be a major concern, local real estate professionals can often provide good advice about the styles and locations of houses most likely to hold or increase their value.

Develop a feel for the neighborhood. Look at other houses on the street. Are they the same general type and with the same quality as the house you are considering? Is the degree of maintenance and exterior landscaping consistent with your plans? Many real estate experts say that the location is by far the most important consideration when buying a property. It is often said that it is wiser to buy one of the cheaper houses on a street and then improve it to add value, than to buy one of the most expensive houses, which cannot be cost-effectively improved.

Also look for trends in the general topography of the land. Is the house at the top of a hill? On a side hill lot? In a low-lying area likely to collect water runoff? A house situated on a hillside can be susceptible to excessive building settlement. A house located in a valley is more likely to have flooding problems.

LANDSCAPING

Upon arriving at the house, look first at the lot itself. Trees generally add value to a property and may help to heat and cool the house. Deciduous trees on the south and west sides shade the building during the summer months yet allow beneficial solar heat gain during the winter. Evergreens on the north side of a building serve as a windbreak to reduce winter heat loss. Look at the condition of the trees. Dead trees may be expensive to remove, especially where access is difficult. Tree limbs overhanging a building can cause damage to the roof and gutters. The abrasive action of branches and leaves on a roof membrane is considerable. Leaves and twigs can clog gutters, causing them to deteriorate rapidly. Branches should be trimmed well away from the building.

Where large trees are close to the building, roots may damage foundation walls and clog drainage pipes or plumbing lines. Some kinds of trees—willows, poplars, and cedars, for example—require large amounts of water and their presence may indicate a high water table. Some trees that grow very quickly, such as poplars, aspens, willows, and elms, can cause settling problems in houses by withdrawing moisture from the soil below the foundations. This problem is most severe in areas with clay soil where considerable swelling and shrinkage occurs with changes in moisture content.

Look at the surface drainage immediately adjacent to the building. It is important that the ground slopes down from the house to prevent rainwater pooling against the exterior foundation walls. Wet basements are often the result of improper exterior grading. Look for a slope of at least one inch per foot for the first six feet away from the building.

FIGURE 1.1 *Swales*

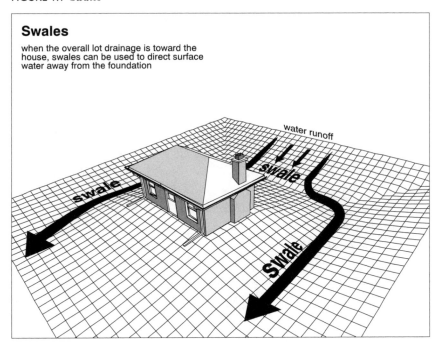

Swales

when the overall lot drainage is toward the
house, swales can be used to direct surface
water away from the foundation

Where one section of the yard slopes toward the house, it may be necessary to create a swale (a gentle trough), as shown in Figure 1.1, that allows water to drain away from the building. Driveways, sidewalks, and
patios should also slope down from the house. Incorrect sloping on
these hard surfaces may be more serious because very little water is absorbed. Poor-draining soils, such as clays, also present more problems
than sandy soils. Sometimes houses are too close together to enjoy opti-
mum drainage. In this case, a V-shaped depression is desirable between
the houses.

Many homes have a perimeter drainage pipe system around the bottom of the foundation walls to collect water standing outside the basement. If the house is more than 25 years old, however, chances are good
that the drainage pipe is nonexistent or has been broken or clogged.
Thus, on older houses, grading is particularly important.

Look at features such as fences, porches, and decks. Are they in
good repair? Will they require frequent maintenance? Look closely at
the wood/soil contact areas for evidence of rot or termite attack. Check
the lawns and gardens. A yard with some bare patches may not be a

problem, although a very uneven surface may have to be worked extensively to yield an attractive lawn. Look at retaining walls, which are expensive to rebuild. These walls should lean slightly into a hill rather than away from it. Also, look near the bottom of the walls for openings (weep holes) that allow water to escape from behind the walls.

GARAGES

Garages should be looked at from both a functional and an aesthetic viewpoint. Verify that the garage is large enough for your needs and that the garage door is operable. Check the roof for leaks and wood-frame garages for rot and termite activity. Also assess the appearance of the garage. When in poor repair, it will detract from the desirability and value of the entire property. And if the garage has to be replaced, this can be an expensive project.

Attached garages commonly found on modern homes are very convenient, but they can pose a safety hazard because carbon monoxide fumes from an automobile can enter the house. In an attached garage, one should look for a gasproof wall and ceiling covering on the garage and a fireproof door into the house. There should also be a step up from the garage into the house or, at the very least, a curb at the doorway. All garages should have a floor drain or a slope to allow water to run out of the garage.

The garage door is usually the largest moving component in a house. The door should open smoothly, with a minimum amount of effort. If properly adjusted, the door will stay halfway open when it is let go in that position. Motorized garage door openers should be tested to make sure that they function properly. The opener should stop and reverse direction if it encounters an obstacle, such as a two-inch block of wood (see Figure 1.2). Keep one hand on the release cord while performing this test; an improperly adjusted opener may damage the door, or the opener itself, if it does not reverse in time. Newer openers also use an electric eye near the bottom of the door to sense objects blocking the path of the door.

Outside sheds are generally considered assets, although they, too, should be examined. Check with local zoning regulations if you are planning to add or move any structure. Often you must obtain a building permit for garages and sheds, and for a number of reasons you may not be

FIGURE 1.2 *Testing Automatic Reverse*

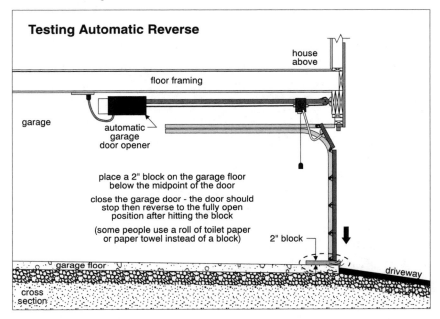

able to obtain a permit. It is best to be sure that one can rebuild before tearing down any outbuilding.

Check the type and condition of the driveway. While concrete driveways are better than asphalt, both are expensive to replace. Look, too, at the slope of the driveway. Consider water runoff and possible problem areas for snow accumulation. The driveway width is usually less than ideal on older houses, and where the driveway passes between two houses, one should be sure there is enough room for a large car or a minivan. Lastly, check whether the driveway is private or shared.

CHIMNEYS

Because a chimney can be properly inspected only from up close, someone will have to climb up onto the roof. If you are going to do this yourself, never use the chimney to pull yourself up or lean against it for this can be very dangerous. In fact, where access is at all difficult, leave the inspection to a roofer or chimney expert and content yourself with doing a preliminary inspection with the aid of binoculars.

From the ground, binoculars will allow you to assess the general condition of the chimney. Keep in mind that a neglected chimney can pose a safety hazard and should be repaired promptly. If you see gaps in the mortar, repointing (scraping out the loose mortar and adding new) will be necessary. Missing bricks or a leaning chimney may mean that the chimney will have to be torn down and rebuilt. In some cases, you will notice that the brickwork is covered with a skim coat of cement (parging). This is a short-term solution that covers up rather than cures the problem of missing bricks or loose mortar. The parging often develops cracks that allow water in behind. Freeze/thaw action will cause the parging to break down quickly.

A cap, usually made of concrete, should be provided at the top of the chimney. This prevents water from entering the masonry there. A cracked cap will allow moisture into the brickwork, which will lead to rapid deterioration. The cap should overhang the brick to allow water to drop off the chimney cap rather than to run down the side of the brick.

Look closely at the flashing (a material, usually metal, which covers the joint between the roof and chimney). This is a common area for leakage and, while not an expensive area to repair, can cause considerable damage if unattended. A good flashing job usually employs a metal such as galvanized steel while roofing cement or tar alone indicates a low-quality job. Wide chimneys present more problems because of the large valleys formed between the upper sides of the chimneys and the roof. Where chimneys are more than 30 inches wide, saddles, or crickets, should be provided (see Figure 1.3). These are deflectors that prevent water or snow accumulation in the valley behind the chimney.

Check the chimney height in relation to the building. A chimney should be at least three feet tall and two feet higher than anything within ten feet horizontally. If you are climbing onto the roof, look down the flues to verify that they are clean and open. Where two or more flues are in one chimney, make sure they are separated. In old unlined chimneys, the brick between the flues is often missing near the top. Where a flue liner is provided, it should extend at least two inches above the cap.

Finally, note the number and location of chimney flues. A separate flue is usually required for each furnace or fireplace. Many older houses were built with one flue serving two fireplaces or a stove and a fireplace.

FIGURE 1.3 *Chimney Saddle Flashings*

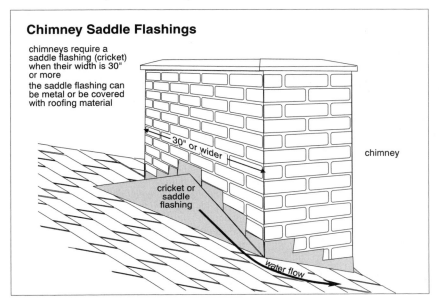

Chimney Saddle Flashings

chimneys require a saddle flashing (cricket) when their width is 30" or more

the saddle flashing can be metal or be covered with roofing material

30" or wider

cricket or saddle flashing

chimney

water flow

When looking at attached or row houses, be careful not to count the neighbor's flue as your own. Often, two flues travel up one chimney on the center wall between the houses, each flue serving the furnace from one house. An unused chimney can be removed down to the roof level to reduce maintenance and repair costs. Many older houses have a chimney that once served a wood stove in the kitchen. This is very often not in use and can easily be removed.

Chimneys can be expensive to repair or rebuild, particularly if they are high or if access is difficult. Scaffolding may have to be erected, which adds to the cost. Save yourself unexpected repair or replacement cost by checking the chimney before you buy.

ROOFS

Roof coverings fulfill three functions on most houses. First, they prevent moisture from penetrating into the top of the house. Second, the overhang on the roof helps protect exterior walls from becoming excessively wet. Third, the roofing system should be aesthetically appealing, consistent with the architecture of the house.

FIGURE 1.4 *Roof Slopes*

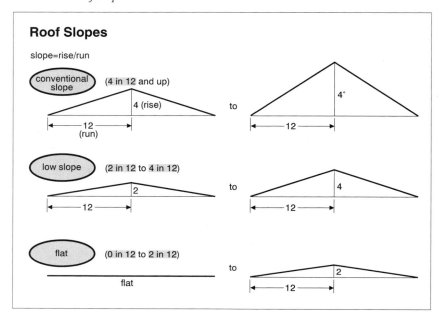

It is often impractical for a potential buyer to get up on a roof, but most sloped roofs can be seen relatively well from ground level with binoculars. We will discuss the various roofing materials individually later in this section. First, however, certain common points should be checked with any roof covering.

The weakest areas on any roof are at changes in direction or materials. Look closely where chimneys, vents, plumbing stacks, and television antennas penetrate the roof membrane. Roof edges and roof/wall intersections should also receive particular attention. Valleys created where different roof angles come together are other problem areas. A flashing of either metal or roll roofing is typically used. Look at the condition of the flashing and the point where the flashing goes under the shingles. People walking on the roof often cause damage by stepping on the flashing. It is usually better to walk on the shingles, wherever possible.

An important roofing term is *pitch*. The pitch, or slope, of a roof (see Figure 1.4) is measured by the number of feet of vertical rise for every 12 feet of horizontal run. Thus, a "4-in-12 roof" would be one that rises 4 feet vertically for every 12 horizontal feet.

FIGURE 1.5 *Ice Dams*

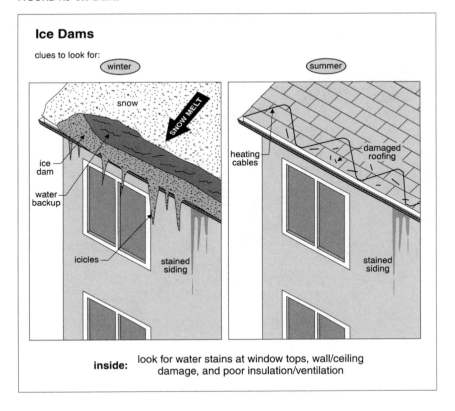

Ice Dams

clues to look for:

winter   summer

snow

SNOW MELT

ice dam

water backup

heating cables

damaged roofing

icicles   stained siding   stained siding

inside: look for water stains at window tops, wall/ceiling damage, and poor insulation/ventilation

Low-sloped roofs with overhangs are susceptible to ice dam problems. Ice damming (as shown in Figure 1.5) is the result of snow accumulation on the roof and is more common on poorly insulated houses. After a snowfall, heat will escape from the house into the attic, melting the snow on the roof. The water will run down and encounter the snow on the roof overhang. Snow in this area has not melted because there is no attic below: consequently, there is no heat. The water runoff encountering this snow will freeze, forming a dam at the lower edge of the roof. Additional water coming down will meet this dam and be collected. This water can then back up underneath the shingles, resulting in damage below. Protection can be afforded by roofing paper, roofing felts, or plastic sheeting laid over the lower sections of the roof prior to application of the shingles. Another solution is the application of electric heating cables on the lower edge of the roof. A well-insulated and ventilated attic will help reduce ice dam problems.

FIGURE 1.6 *Typical Asphalt Shingle Application–Showing Metal Drip Edge*

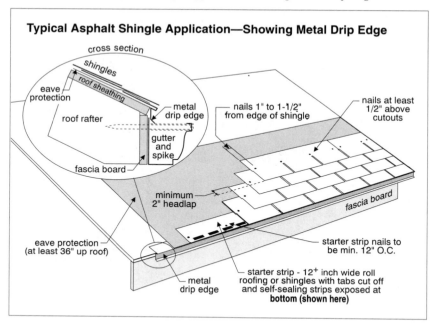

Asphalt Shingles

Asphalt shingles are the most common type of roofing used across North America over the past 40 years. Asphalt shingles are used both on new houses and as retrofit material on older homes (see Figure 1.6). The shingle itself is comprised of fiberglass, paper, or felt impregnated with asphalt and covered with small granules. The mineral granules reflect the ultraviolet rays of the sun, preventing breakdown of the asphalt. Most modern shingles last approximately 15 years, although higher-quality shingles can last 25 years.

Several clues show up when an asphalt roof is wearing out. Watch for missing granules, which appear as bare spots on the shingles. A large accumulation of granules in the gutters also indicates that the roof is getting old. Shingles that buckle in the middle or curl at the edges have very little life remaining. Torn or missing shingles mean that immediate repairs are necessary.

Because of exposure to the sun, the south and west sides of a roof age more rapidly. Also, the bottom shingles, which receive more water runoff than do upper sections, tend to wear out first. Look closely, then, at the lower shingles on the south and west sides of the roof. As mentioned earlier, the abrasive action of overhanging tree limbs can also damage a roof, so be on the lookout for this situation.

The minimum pitch for most shingle roofs is 4-in-12. Make sure the slope is at least this much. Special "low slope" shingles can be used down to 2-in-12, but these are not common. On roofs with a pitch of less than 2-in-12, asphalt shingles should never be used.

Where reroofing is necessary, it is important to determine how many layers of shingles are on the roof. Ideally, no more than two layers of roofing material should be provided. Additional materials result in an uneven surface and, more important, excessive weight on the roof framing members. By looking at the edges of a roof, it is usually possible to determine how many layers of shingles there are. If there are already two layers or more, the roof should be stripped prior to reroofing. This will also provide an opportunity to examine the roof boards below and make any necessary repairs.

Slates

Slate roofs are found primarily on older houses and, because of their cost, are not widely used in modern construction. Slate shingles are heavy, brittle, and may be many colors, depending on where they are quarried. These roofs are considered high quality and can last 100 years or more, with good maintenance. Good slates deteriorate only slightly because of freeze/thaw action, but they are susceptible to mechanical damage. The most common problem is rusting of the nails holding the slates in place. As the nails rust, the slates slip out of position, allowing water to penetrate the roofing system. Additional water accelerates the rusting of adjacent nails and the roof begins to deteriorate quickly.

Generally considered aesthetically pleasing, a slate roof will often add value to a property. However, slate roofs do require a good deal of regular attention and are costly to maintain. Slate roof maintenance and repair are generally not for the do-it-yourselfer.

Look carefully for broken or missing slates that have slipped out of position. Low-quality slates will be flaking off in layers. Again, it is important to examine all joints in the roofing system including the valleys and ridges. If only a few slates require resecuring or replacing, the roof can probably be repaired. If more than 15 to 20 have been damaged or are missing, it may be best to provide a new roof surface. Where a slate roof can be saved, it is generally worthwhile to do so. Where a complete new roof is necessary, the slate roof is usually replaced with asphalt shingles. A word of caution: Do not walk on slate roofs. A slate roof is typically very steep with a pitch of 6-in-12, or more. Slates are very slippery and, if the nails are badly rusted, can easily be dislodged by the pressure of the footsteps. Slate roofs should be examined from the ground with binoculars or from an adjacent roof.

Wood Shingles and Shakes

Whether redwood, cedar, or pine, wood roof coverings are made of machine-cut shingles of uniform shape and thickness, or rough hand-split shakes of varying dimensions. While very attractive, wood roofs are less common than asphalt shingles because of their cost. They are also prohibited in some places because they are fire hazards, unless the wood has been chemically treated. Well-maintained, properly installed wood roofs can last 39 to 50 years; however, the newer practice of installing wood roofs over plywood sheathing can reduce their life to as little as 10 years. This reduced life span is caused by the lack of air circulation on the underside of the roof, which the older, spaced sheathing allowed. The reduced air circulation does not allow the wood roof to dry out properly. The pitch should not be less than 4-in-12, and, generally speaking, the steeper the roof, the more weatherproof it will be and the longer it will last.

While not as weathertight as asphalt roofing, wood shingles do swell when wet, to provide a tighter seal. In addition to looking for split, cupped, curled (as shown in Figure 1.7), or missing shingles, one should look for evidence of rot, particularly on the lower shingles. The north or shaded sides of a roof do not dry as quickly and are more prone to rot. Sometimes a moss or a fungus can be seen, which is evidence of excessive moisture. The moss can force the shingles apart, allowing wind-driven rain to penetrate the roofing system. Look for good attic ventilation, which will help the wood dry quickly after a rain.

Repair is usually only practical where a few isolated shingles need replacement. A deteriorated wood shingle roof can often be covered with one layer of asphalt shingles. Wood shakes should be stripped prior

FIGURE 1.7 *Curling, Cupping, and Splitting Wood Shingles*

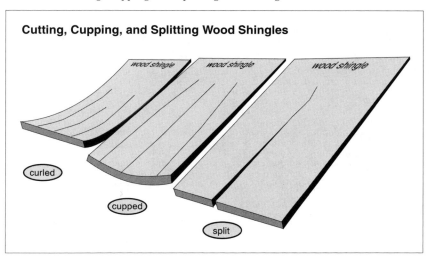

to reroofing, because of the uneven surface created by the roof overlay. Again, where possible, avoid walking on a wood roof.

Wood shingles are also often used as a siding material where they have a longer life than on a roof because of the better weatherproofness afforded by the vertical installation and the protection from wetting provided by the roof overhang.

Fiber Cement Shingles

These high-quality shingles are made of a mixture of portland cement and asbestos fiber or another type of fiber. They are much more expensive than asphalt shingles and thus less commonly used. Better-quality shingles have a higher fiber content. While the shingles are brittle and susceptible to mechanical damage, they have a high fire resistance and a life expectancy of up to 50 years.

Fiber cement shingles are applied on roofs with a pitch of 3-in-12 or more. Difficulties include broken, cracked, and missing shingles and problems at the joints. Replacement, again, is usually with asphalt shingles and should be done after stripping the roof. Fiber cement shingles are also used as a siding and can provide a very durable surface.

FIGURE 1.8 *Built-Up Roofing Membrane–4-Ply*

Built-Up Roofing Membrane—4-Ply

gravel

flood coat of asphalt

exposure=9"

note:

for 3-ply exposure=12"

36"

roofing felts (36" wide)

for 2-ply exposure=18"

hot asphalt

base layer of felt (dry laid) with minimum 2" overlap at edges

downward slope of roof

roof sheathing

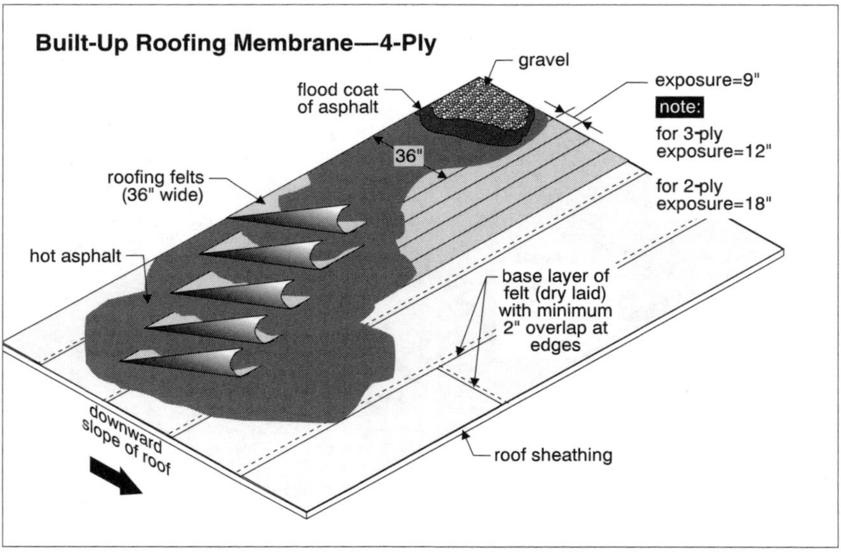

Selvage or Roll Roofing

This material is made of papers or felts, impregnated with asphalt and covered with stone granules, not unlike asphalt shingles. It comes in rolls, typically 19 to 36 inches wide. The material is laid in strips and nailed to the roofing boards. This is a low-quality roof covering with a normal life expectancy of five to ten years. It is frequently found on porches, garages, and small additions. When examining roll roofing, look for missing granules, evidence of buckling, lifted seams, and exposed nail heads. The seams and nail heads should be covered with tar to prevent leakage at these points. This material is sometimes used on a flat roof, although it still provides a low-quality roof with a short life expectancy.

Built-Up Roofs

A high-quality flat roof covering is a built-up roof system (see Figure 1.8) sometimes called a tar and gravel roof. This system consists of several layers of roofing felts (paper impregnated with asphalt) laid in an overlapping membrane with coats of asphalt between. A final coat of asphalt is applied, then covered with a gravel topping. The felts and asphalt provide the waterproof membrane and the gravel reflects the sun's rays, protects the roof from mechanical damage, and improves fire resistance.

The roof may consist of two, three, four, or five plies and with a good installation may have a life expectancy of 15 to 20 years. Because of the many steps involved, there is considerable potential for error in the construction of flat roof coverings. They are expensive to install and can be high-maintenance areas. Leaks in a flat roof are often difficult to locate, although, as with other roofs, the joints are the weakest areas.

The term *flat roof* is somewhat misleading, for all roofs should slope slightly to allow water runoff. When inspecting a flat roof, look for areas where water may pond, because this will shorten the life considerably. Bubbles, blisters, and splits in the membrane indicate that repairs will soon be needed. Where the gravel is missing, and the membrane is exposed, deterioration will be rapid. The maximum slope for a gravel-covered built-up roof is usually three in twelve. Steeper slopes will result in a loss of gravel and cold flow of the asphalt.

Sometimes a built-up roof system is applied without the protective gravel layer. This is not a good situation and the life expectancy of the roof is significantly reduced. Should the membrane be in reasonably good condition, it is possible to pour a flood coat of asphalt and add the gravel.

Where a wood deck has been laid over a flat roof, it will not be necessary to add gravel. In this situation, the wood decking will protect the membrane. However, when a deck has been installed, try to get a good look at the roofing below. When that membrane wears out, it will be expensive to lift up the entire wood deck to make repairs.

As with other roof systems, one should not apply a new roof over old ones indiscriminately. The weight of a built-up roof is considerable. Also water is often trapped in the old roof membrane. A new covering will seal in that moisture. On a hot day, the water will evaporate and can bubble the new roof as it tries to escape. While small repairs can often be undertaken by the homeowner, replacing a flat roof is not usually a good project for the amateur.

Modified Bitumen

Many newer flat roofs are covered with a polymer-modified asphalt membrane, often called rubberized asphalt. This material comes in rolls and is usually either torched down or mopped to the roof using hot asphalt. The membrane may be protected from the sun using granules similar to those on asphalt shingles, silver-colored reflective paint, or nothing at all. In some areas, it is common to install these roofs with a single layer of membrane; in other areas, a double layer is typical.

Modified bitumen roofs are also considered high-quality systems. In many cases, roof replacement is needed because of defects in the installation or the flashings, not because of failure of the material itself. Modified bitumen membranes often last 15-to-20 years.

Specialty Roofing Materials

Several specialty roofs are available and a number of new materials are always under development. Some of the more common systems will be touched on here.

A Spanish tile or clay tile roof is attractive and long-lasting, but it is expensive to install and to maintain. The tiles are brittle and very susceptible to mechanical damage.

Metal roofs are used on both sloped and flat roofs. A sloped metal roof can be a series of ribbed metal panels or metal shingles. The metals used include galvanized steel and various tin alloys. This type of roofing is more common in rural areas and is susceptible to rusting, particularly at the joints. Flat metal roofs are usually painted and are quite durable if kept covered.

Concrete tile roofs with life expectancies of 50 years and more are popular in some areas. This roofing system is designed to look like Spanish tile and is suitable for sloped roofs. Because the concrete tile is very heavy, the roof structure must be designed specifically to carry the additional load.

There are several single-ply roofing membranes, usually in sheet form, which are used on both flat and sloped roofs. Some of these materials are rubber-based while others are plastic.

REROOFING

Where reroofing is necessary, it is important to determine how many layers of roofing are present. As discussed, no more than two layers should be provided. Stripping a roof prior to resurfacing typically increases an already expensive job 30 to 50 percent, although in some cases the cost can be doubled.

GUTTERS AND DOWNSPOUTS

The gutter and downspout system is designed to collect rainwater and melted snow from the roof and discharge it to a safe location. Typically, water is directed underground into a storm sewer or onto the lawn surface well away from the house. A splash block should be provided where the downspout discharges onto the lawn to prevent erosion, and the discharge point should be at least six feet from the building.

While gutters and downspouts are relatively inexpensive to install and maintain, they can cause serious damage if neglected. Many wet basement problems result from downspouts that deposit water in one spot immediately adjacent to the house. Improperly aligned gutters can collect water and allow it to back up, damaging the woodwork of the roof and the eaves. Soil erosion problems are also common where gutters are in disrepair or are missing.

Gutters should be sized in accordance with the roof area (see Figure 1.9). While four-inch-wide systems are common, five-inch gutters usually perform much better for a slightly increased cost. Downspouts should be provided every 30 to 40 feet along the gutters. On steep roofs, splash guards may be needed at the bottom of roof valleys to prevent water overshooting the gutters. The gutters should slope towards the downspouts so that water can drain completely. The gutters must also be kept clear of debris because water trapped by leaves, for example, will accelerate deterioration of the gutter. Screening is available that, if properly installed and maintained, can be effective in keeping gutters clear.

FIGURE 1.9 *Gutter and Downspout Installation*

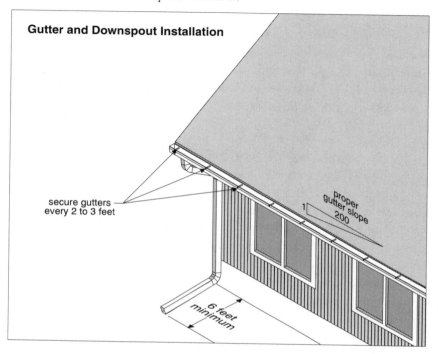

Types of Gutters

Galvanized gutters are still the most common kind, although they need to be painted every three to five years. Unless exceptionally well maintained, galvanized gutters and downspouts last approximately 20 years. Ideally, they should be painted on the inside as well as on the outside and bare metal must be appropriately primed before painting. There are also enameled steel and vinyl-coated steel gutters, which do not require regular painting. These, of course, are slightly more expensive than the bare metal ones.

Aluminum gutters are competitive with galvanized gutters in terms of cost. The baked-on enamel finish does not require regular painting. Another advantage is that they can readily be formed and cut to length on-site, reducing the number of joints. Aluminum does not rust as galvanized steel does, but the aluminum is not as strong. Aluminum gutters are susceptible to damage from ladders leaned against them. Leaking at the seams is also a common problem, but one that is easily overcome.

The joint sealer should be a flexible compound that can move with the expansion and contraction of the metal. Under normal circumstances, aluminum gutters should last 20 to 30 years.

Copper gutters are probably the best available and can last the lifetime of the house. Typically, they are not painted and thus turn the characteristic green or brown of oxidized copper. Copper gutters are several times more expensive than galvanized or aluminum ones and are not commonly used residentially today.

If the house has copper gutters and downspouts, particular attention should be given to keeping gutters clear and properly aligned. When copper gutters are painted, it is difficult to distinguish them from galvanized steel. Scratching away some of the paint and oxidization should show a shiny copper finish. Alternatively, a magnet can be used to determine what type the gutters are. Galvanized steel will attract a magnet, but copper and aluminum will not.

Wood gutters are sometimes found on older houses and may even be integral to the roofing system. Usually found on houses of superior quality, these can provide very good service if well maintained. If allowed to deteriorate, however, they can be very expensive to repair or replace. Some wood gutters are lined with lead or copper, which increases their durability.

Plastic gutters are made of the newest material available. Many plastic gutter systems are geared to the do-it-yourselfer. Their light weight, ease of connection, and low maintenance make this a very appealing alternative for the home handyman. On the other hand, plastic gutters are available in a limited range of colors and the plastic may become brittle in the winter and subject to splitting. Plastic gutters are also easily damaged by the weight of a person climbing a ladder. Another concern is that the material's high coefficient of expansion may lead to seam problems over time.

Inspection

When inspecting, ensure that gutters are provided where necessary, including on porches, flat roofs, and dormers. If in doubt whether gutters are necessary in one area, check similar houses on the street for a pattern.

FIGURE 1.10 *Gutters–Common Reasons for Leakage*

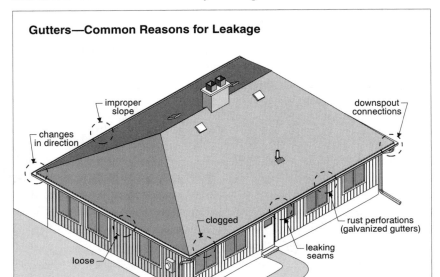

Gutters—Common Reasons for Leakage

To check for leakage problems, look for debris accumulation in the gutters and for evidence of leaks (see Figure 1.10) such as rust on the underside of the gutters. Watch for discoloration of the eaves or exterior walls. Dark streaks on the outside of the gutters, or fascia boards, indicate overflowing water. Check that the gutters slope slightly to the downspouts. If possible, look at the inside of the gutters for evidence of rust or other deterioration. If rusting problems are minor, or small holes are noted, a number of patching materials, such as roofing cement, will help extend the life of the gutters.

Check for adequate downspouts, keeping in mind the area of the roof served by each length of gutter. Follow the downspouts to grade level and determine where the water is discharged. Tap the downspouts to see if they are clogged. When underground piping leading to storm sewers is blocked or broken, it may be easiest to redirect the water onto the lawn using a splash block.

While gutters and downspouts should not weigh heavily in the buying decision, they may be the source of serious problems and do indicate the quality of general maintenance.

FIGURE 1.11 *Wall Assemblies*

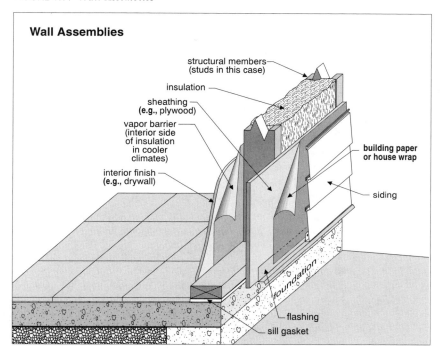

Exterior Wall Finishes

A good exterior finish acts as a weatherproof skin on a house. It should provide a low maintenance surface that is attractive and consistent with the style of the home. A good exterior finish should also breathe, allowing evaporated moisture to pass through the wall. Most houses are either solid masonry or wood-frame construction. In solid masonry, the structural members may also form the exterior finish. This is true in brick walls, concrete walls, and stone walls. In most other cases, the exterior finish, or siding, is applied over the wood frame and does not figure significantly in the structural integrity.

On wood-frame construction, a sheathing (see Figure 1.11) is attached to the two-by-four or two-by-six wood studs. For many years, this sheathing was wooden boards nailed onto the studs covered with tar paper or house wrap. More recently, the sheathing consists of fiberboard with a surface coating of tar. This sheathing provides a subsurface to which the siding can be secured. It also adds to the weatherproofness of the house and enhances structural rigidity to some degree. The sheathing should breathe to allow the passage of water vapor. In some modern construction, sheathing may be plywood, waferboard, or rigid insulation board. As energy efficiency becomes more important, this practice will probably become more common.

Some of the materials commonly used for siding include brick, lumber, wood shingles, and shakes, plywood, particleboard, stucco, asphalt shingles, insulbrick, fiber cement shingles, artificial stone, aluminum, vinyl, and steel. When inspecting an exterior wall finish, keep in mind that its weatherproofness is most important. Look for weakness at joints, such as windows and door openings, and along the top and bottom of walls. Look at outside corners and other areas where mechanical damage is likely. Ensure that the protective coating present (for example, paint or stain) is in good condition and covers the entire surface. Look closely below windows. Surface tension causes water to collect here and deterioration will often be most noticeable in this area.

Siding materials such as wood are susceptible to moisture damage and should not be carried down to grade level. These sidings should terminate at least eight inches above the ground.

Condensation Problems

Condensation problems within exterior walls can occur during the winter months. Warm, moist air from inside the house enters the wall cavity. As colder surfaces are encountered close to the outer skin, the air will deposit its moisture on whatever surface is available. Vapor diffusion also contributes to the problem. Here, no air movement is necessary. A difference in vapor pressures can cause moisture within the house to migrate into the wall system. Again, condensation is the result. Ventilated exterior siding materials help reduce wall condensation problems. Vaportight skins worsen the situation.

Condensation problems show up on wood siding as blistered or peeling paint and rotting wood. Masonry may spall (crumble or flake) as a result of freeze/thaw action. Sidings, such as steel, aluminum, and vinyl, may not show any evidence of a problem behind the wall. This, of course, is the least desirable situation for damage can go unnoticed for some time.

A newly insulated wall may be very susceptible to condensation damage, particularly if a good vapor barrier has not been provided on the warm side of the insulation. Here the exterior siding, which used to be heated by the air in the house, becomes a cold surface on which condensation can readily form. The insulation also reduces the natural ventilation in the wall cavity.

Preventive or corrective actions are fairly simple if the problem is diagnosed early. Interior wall surfaces can be covered with a vapor-barrier paint, and air leakage into the walls can be reduced by caulking and sealing interruptions in the interior wall surface. Exterior surfaces can also be better ventilated to carry away the moisture before it condenses.

Brick

Brick on the outside of a house may constitute part of solid masonry construction or may be a veneer over a wood frame (see Figure 1.12). Look for gaps in the mortar between the bricks. Gaps are often most noticeable in areas where water has passed over the brick for some time, eroding the mortar. Check, too, for openings between the brick and the wood framing around doors and windows. Look closely at the top of the brick where the roof or eaves come in contact. Once again, we are looking for a weatherproof seal at these joints.

Moisture trapped behind the brick can lead to spalling. Mortar joints should ideally be slightly recessed with a concave surface. Where mortar is missing, or crumbling, it will have to be chiseled out and replaced (repointed).

Examine a brick wall for evidence of settling or sloping, or the wall pulling away from the framing. These can be very serious problems requiring reconstruction of the entire wall. Look closely at cracks in the brickwork. While diagonal hairline cracks above and below windows usually are not serious, cracks that go through the wall to the inside, or which widen to one-quarter inch or more, can be. Cracks that have been repaired several times are another clue to trouble. Refer to Chapter 2 for comments on masonry cracking.

Old brick walls with many coats of paint or a heavy accumulation of dirt are often sandblasted. This is usually bad for the brick and the results may be severe spalling and rapid deterioration. Glazed bricks are like a loaf of bread. The outer crust is very hard, but the inner part

FIGURE 1.12 *Veneer versus Solid Masonry*

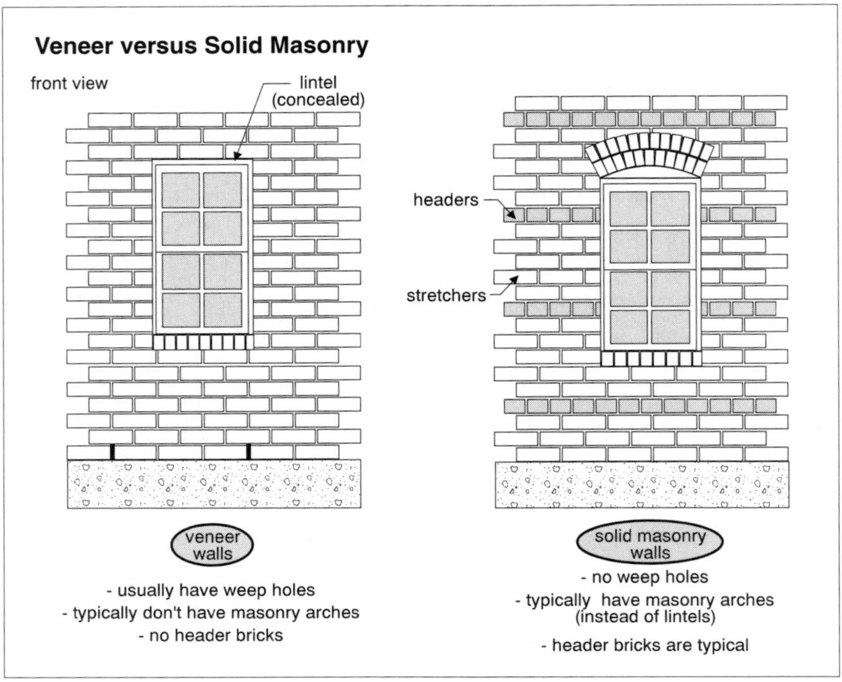

is relatively soft. When the crust is removed by sandblasting, the brick becomes very soft and porous. In some cases, sealants such as silicone are applied to the brick after sandblasting. This attempt to stop water penetration into the brick can cause problems. Moisture coming from inside the house can be trapped behind this plastic skin on the outer surface of the brick where it can freeze, expand, and lead to even more rapid deterioration. An alternative to sandblasting is chemical cleaning. This often is more satisfactory and, generally speaking, is easier on the brickwork.

Vines on a wall can lead to damage for the vines tend to trap water near the surface of the wall. Damage to the mortar may occur over a period of time. The deterioration is generally slow, however, and not usually a major problem. It should be understood that with vegetation immediately adjacent to wall surfaces, insects and pests find easy access into a house.

A brick wall in disrepair can be covered with a new siding material. Stucco is often used with satisfactory results. It is important, however,

FIGURE 1.13 *Stucco–Three-Coat Process*

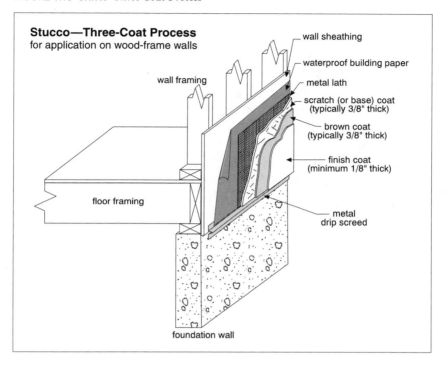

to ensure that damage to the brick below will not be progressive—that is, that it will not continue to deteriorate under the new siding.

Stucco

Stucco is essentially a mixture of sand, lime, and cement that is troweled onto a wall over wood or wire lath in two or three coats. It may be applied over masonry or frame walls (see Figure 1.13). Usually it is possible to tell what the stucco is applied over by tapping the wall. Stucco over masonry sounds much more solid than stucco does over wood-frame walls. Stucco finishes can be painted many colors and some have a stone aggregate embedded in the surface for aesthetic reasons. Stucco applied over frame tends to show more hairline cracking caused by the movement of the wood framing. Cracks that appear in stucco must be promptly repaired. Otherwise, water gets behind the stucco causing rapid deterioration of the lath, sheathing, and framing. Once again, look for weaknesses at joints and intersections. Looks can be deceiving with stucco: A wall that seems to be in poor repair may only need minor patching and a new coat of paint. Where wood is used as a surface material with stucco, as in a Tudor-style home, make sure the wood is sound. Water allowed to collect, especially at end grains or on horizontal wood edges, can cause damage not only to the wood on the surface, but to the substructures behind.

While damaged areas of the stucco can be repaired, it is difficult to match texture and color. Often an entire wall has to be repainted after patching. Be careful to use a stucco mix similar to the one that is in place. Dissimilar mixes used in patches may lead to chronic cracking as a result of differential rates of expansion and contraction.

Synthetic Stucco

There is a new type of stucco that is quite different from hard-coat stucco. This stucco is commonly part of Exterior Insulating Finishing Systems (EIFS). An EIFS wall (see Figure 1.14) consists of a wood-framed wall, which is sheathed in the normal fashion. Sheets of polystyrene insulation are fastened to the wall. A glass fiber mesh is applied to the insulation and a base coat of polymer-modified stucco is sprayed or troweled on. This layer is much thinner than conventional stucco. When this has dried, the finish coat of stucco is applied. The two layers of stucco together are approximately ³/₁₆-inch thick.

This material was originally designed for use in dry climates, such as the American Southwest. In wetter climates, this material is somewhat controversial. While the surface of the material is quite waterproof, penetrations through the walls often leak, allowing water to get behind the stucco. Once behind the stucco, the water is often trapped, which can cause rot inside the wall. Newer installations may allow for drainage of this water. Unfortunately, one cannot determine the true extent of any damage without removing the wall finishes. It is very important to inspect around all windows, doors, and other penetrations to ensure that they are completely sealed against water penetration.

Across North America, there have been cases of banks refusing mortgages on EIFS homes, restrictions on the installation of EIFS, and class-action lawsuits launched against manufacturers of EIFS. Needless to say, it is best to find out the history of this material in your area. If

FIGURE 1.14 *Synthetic Stucco (EIFS)*

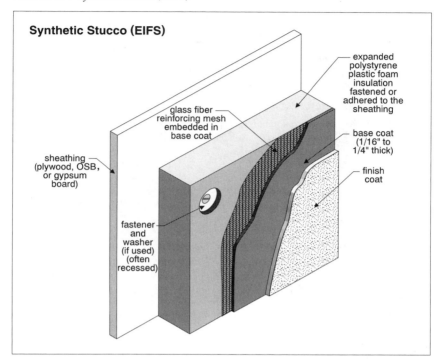

Synthetic Stucco (EIFS)

expanded polystyrene plastic foam insulation fastened or adhered to the sheathing

glass fiber reinforcing mesh embedded in base coat

base coat (1/16" to 1/4" thick)

sheathing (plywood, OSB, or gypsum board)

finish coat

fastener and washer (if used) (often recessed)

the house you are considering has an EIFS exterior finish, you can also obtain a specialist's evaluation.

Boards

Boards may be installed horizontally (such as clapboard) as shown in Figure 1.15, vertically (board and batten), or diagonally (tongue and groove). Unless highly weather-resistant woods such as cedar are used, these walls require a paint or stain. It is usually necessary to reapply these protective coatings every three to five years. After repainting several times, it will be necessary to strip off all the paint, for thick coatings can provide a vapor barrier leading to condensation problems.

Look for cracked, warped, and missing boards. In addition to the usual weak areas, check for exposed end grains, which will absorb moisture readily. As discussed earlier, wood siding should terminate at least eight inches above grade level. A common problem with wood siding is

FIGURE 1.15 *Horizontal Wood Siding*

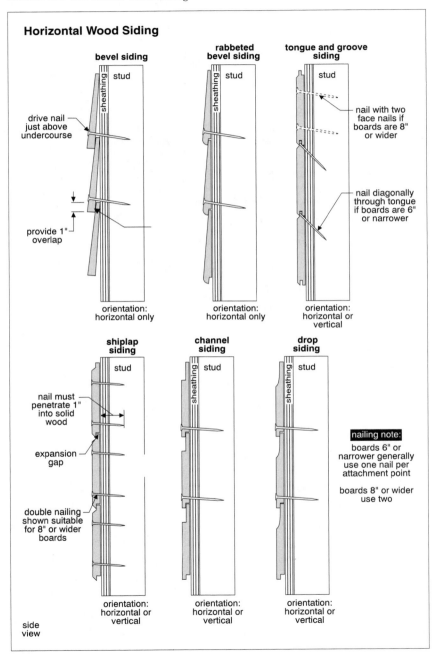

Horizontal Wood Siding

bevel siding

stud

sheathing

drive nail just above undercourse

provide 1" overlap

orientation: horizontal only

rabbeted bevel siding

stud

sheathing

orientation: horizontal only

tongue and groove siding

stud

nail with two face nails if boards are 8" or wider

nail diagonally through tongue if boards are 6" or narrower

orientation: horizontal or vertical

shiplap siding

stud

nail must penetrate 1" into solid wood

expansion gap

double nailing shown suitable for 8" or wider boards

orientation: horizontal or vertical

channel siding

stud

sheathing

orientation: horizontal or vertical

drop siding

stud

sheathing

nailing note:
boards 6" or narrower generally use one nail per attachment point

boards 8" or wider use two

orientation: horizontal or vertical

side view

rust streaking from nails used to hold the siding on. The use of improper nails can spoil the appearance of a complete wall system. The nailing pattern for boards is important. It is possible to fix the boards to the sheathing with too many nails, preventing the natural expansion of the boards. This can lead to premature splitting.

Shingles and Shakes

Often made of cedar, these siding materials are similar to roofing shingles and shakes. They are a good-quality siding material, if properly installed and maintained. They can be left natural, stained, or painted. Check for knots, loose, and shifted shingles, or shingles that have cracked and broken off at the edges. Look for evidence of moss, fungus, or other signs of rot, particularly at the bottom of wall sections.

Wood Panels

Composition materials, such as plywood, chipboard, and waferboard, can be used satisfactorily outside. However, they are not usually considered high-quality finishes, and a small flaw may result in a large unsightly problem. These sidings can be subject to warping and buckling and the layers of the plywood may separate (delaminate). Many sheet goods, such as plywood, do not breathe well and can lead to condensation problems. Once again, exposed edges may absorb water quickly.

Asphalt Shingles and Insulbrick Siding

These low-cost and reasonably durable siding materials became popular in the 1940s. The imitation brick pattern, often referred to as insulbrick, is not generally considered eye-pleasing. Today, it is often replaced simply by covering it with a new siding. Look for the same signs of wear as with asphalt shingles on roofs. Again, the bottom of the wall is a potentially weak area and, ideally, a metal flashing should direct water away from the bottom of the shingles. When repairs are necessary, it is very difficult to match colors. Insulbrick siding is becoming harder to find even for patching purposes.

FIGURE 1.16 *Metal and Vinyl Siding*

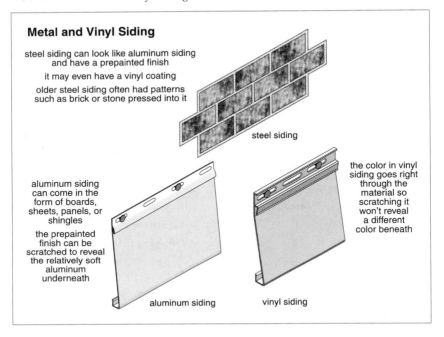

Metal and Vinyl Siding

steel siding can look like aluminum siding
and have a prepainted finish

it may even have a vinyl coating

older steel siding often had patterns
such as brick or stone pressed into it

steel siding

the color in vinyl
siding goes right
through the
material so
scratching it
won't reveal
a different
color beneath

aluminum siding
can come in the
form of boards,
sheets, panels, or
shingles

the prepainted
finish can be
scratched to reveal
the relatively soft
aluminum
underneath

aluminum siding   vinyl siding

Aluminum and Steel Siding

Presently popular as replacement sidings, these materials are relatively inexpensive to install and need little maintenance. They come in
several styles (see Figure 1.16), including traditional horizontal clapboard and vertical board. Sometimes the aluminum is vinyl-covered.
Depending on the siding itself, and on the installation technique, aluminum or steel siding may not breathe well. A good installation includes a backer board that helps the metal resist denting. Insulated
aluminum siding is not cost-effective in some climates, for the amount
of insulation added is relatively small in relation to the added cost.

Individual panels can be replaced, although it may be difficult to
match colors because of weathering. Some sidings can be painted fairly
successfully with specialty paint, but then this becomes a regular maintenance item. Aluminum is also commonly used to cover wood soffits
and fascia and to replace galvanized gutters.

Fiber Cement Shingles or Sheet Siding

Fiber cement shingles or sheet goods are made of the same material as the roofing shingles, although they may be somewhat thinner. This is a reasonably good-quality siding material and can be painted any color. This material is brittle but, generally speaking, quite durable. When inspecting it, look for evidence of broken or cracked shingles.

Vinyl

This product has also become very popular, competing successfully with metal siding. This material can be torn or punctured, and, in some cases, is susceptible to fading problems if proper plastic mixes are not used.

WINDOWS

While there are several different types and qualities of windows, defective windows in a house can be a source of major inconvenience and expense. Windows in disrepair contribute to heat loss, uncomfortable drafts, poor ventilation, and damage to interior and exterior finishes. Because window sizes are not standardized for the most part, repair or replacement is almost always a custom job involving high costs. A complete set of new windows can easily cost more than a roof or heating system can.

Windows should be inspected from both the exterior and the interior. On the exterior, examine the quality of the fit between the window frame and the wall system. Caulking should be provided here. A drip cap at the top of the window frame will direct water away from the window and prevent it from forming a pond at the top of the frame. Also, look for a good slope on the windowsills so that water does not collect against the bottom of the window. On the underside of the sill should be a groove that will prevent water from running along the underside of the sill back to the wall surface. Check for the presence of storm windows on all windows, either fixed or operable, unless additional glazing (more than one pane of glass) has been provided. Look for deterioration of the sashes or frames and for damage to screens. Putty that is

FIGURE 1.17 *Window Well*

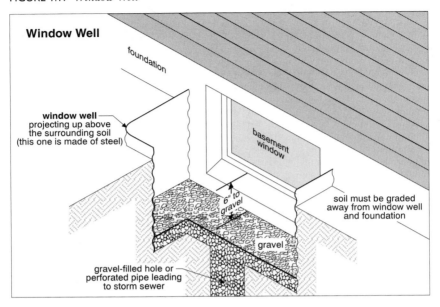

loose or missing will require maintenance, and broken or cracked panes of glass must be replaced.

Note the orientation of windows, for this will affect heating costs. South windows allow the warming winter sunlight in. With west windows, the house becomes hot during the summer months. North and east windows can be areas of high heat loss, depending on prevailing winds.

Look particularly closely at basement windows. Often storm windows are nonexistent here and frames are frequently damaged by moisture. If the basement windows are below grade, there should be a window well (see Figure 1.17) that allows light in and prevents moisture buildup. Look for wood frames on basement windows in direct contact with soil, which could lead to accelerated deterioration of the wood, and in areas where termites are a problem, can provide easy access into the house for these insects.

Window wells should be drained to allow water to discharge. Typically, a French drain comprised of gravel is provided. Where drainage is poor, a plastic dome cover often can be fitted over the window well to direct water away from the window. This, however, prevents outside ventilation when opening the basement windows.

Expect some imperfections when inspecting windows for very few houses have a complete and perfect set. Look rather for trends of recurring deficiencies when going from window to window. Do not clutter your thinking by attempting to note every minor deficiency. We will talk more about windows in Chapter 7.

EXTERIOR DOORS

It may be helpful to think of exterior doors as windows without glass or with very small panes of glass. A door is essentially a hole in your exterior wall, presenting all the problems associated with construction joints and heat loss.

Front doors are generally part of the architecture of the house and should contribute to the overall effect. Unless the door is an insulated core type, however, it should be provided with a storm door in cold climates. The need for a storm door is somewhat reduced when the house layout includes an interior vestibule with a second door. Storm doors help reduce air infiltration and better-quality doors do not camouflage the appeal of the primary door. Storm doors may be made of wood or metal and often double as screen doors, either with a self-storing screen or a replaceable glass insert in the center of the door. Weatherstripping on both the storm and primary door should be well maintained.

Wood exterior doors are available in a wide variety of qualities, including everything from the solid door to a hollow-core, veneer door. The two common styles are a flush type and a rail and stile or panel type. A panel door has raised horizontal, vertical, or diagonal members bracketing recessed panels. Metal doors are available in several styles as well. These doors usually have insulated cores and do not require storms.

Check the width and height of the front door. It should be no less than 32 inches wide and 80 inches high. Generally, larger doors indicate better houses and one can develop a feel for the overall quality just by looking at the original front door.

Locking Mechanisms

Security is a consideration here. When purchasing a resale home, it is often impossible to know whether all keys for existing door locks have been obtained; therefore, it is generally considered prudent to change the locks. In some cases, it is better to add a lock than to sacrifice a high-quality piece of door hardware. Note the location of windowpanes in the door in relation to interior locking mechanisms. If the window is too close to the lock, it will be easy to break the pane and open the door.

SUMMARY

The house exterior often receives less attention than it should. Many outside repairs are put off until they become major expenses. Some of the most costly work includes the following: regrading a yard to improve drainage if much of it is concrete, asphalt, or patio stone; rebuilding a dilapidated garage; rebuilding tall chimneys; replacing roof coverings (especially if the old covering is removed first); repointing large areas of masonry walls; replacing exterior sidings; and adding storm windows. Any of these jobs can run well in excess of $1,000.

CHECKLIST: The Exterior

Landscaping

1. General land slope?

2. Dead trees?

3. Deteriorated fences, porches, decks, or patios?

4. Retaining walls leaning?

5. Garage and driveway condition?

Chimneys

1. How many?

2. Number of flues?

3. Location?

4. Adequate height?

5. Leaning?

6. Mortar condition?

7. Flashing condition?

Roofs

1. Type?

2. Age?

3. Condition?

4. Gutters:
   Complete?
   Sloped properly?
   Leaks?
   Discharge where?

Exterior Wall Finishes

1. General condition?

2. Cracks?

3. Weatherproof?

4. Paint or stain needed?

5. Mortar condition?

Windows

6. Storms provided?

7. Caulking and putty condition?

8. Sill slope and condition?

9. Basement window wells:
      Clear?
      Drains?
      Condition?

Doors

1. Storm provided?

2. Door condition?

3. Weatherstripping?

4. Locking mechanism?

2

THE STRUCTURE

When assessing the structure of a home, it is best to break the structural components into two categories: the exterior structural components and the interior components.

THE EXTERIOR STRUCTURE

The exterior components include the footings on which the foundation walls rest (see Figure 2.1), the foundation walls on which the exterior walls sit, and the exterior walls.

The Footings

Unless the level of the basement floor has been altered, you probably will never get a chance to see the footings for they are underneath the basement walls below the level of the floor. The footings are simply pads, roughly twice the width of the foundation walls, on which the walls sit. Their function is to spread the concentrated load of the foundation walls over a larger area to help prevent the house from settling. The footings, which are usually made of concrete, should lie on undisturbed soil.

FIGURE 2.1 *Overview of House Structure*

Overview of House Structure

collar tie — roof rafter

ceiling joist

bearing wall   exterior wall

floor joist   bearing beam

foundation wall   column

footing

cross section

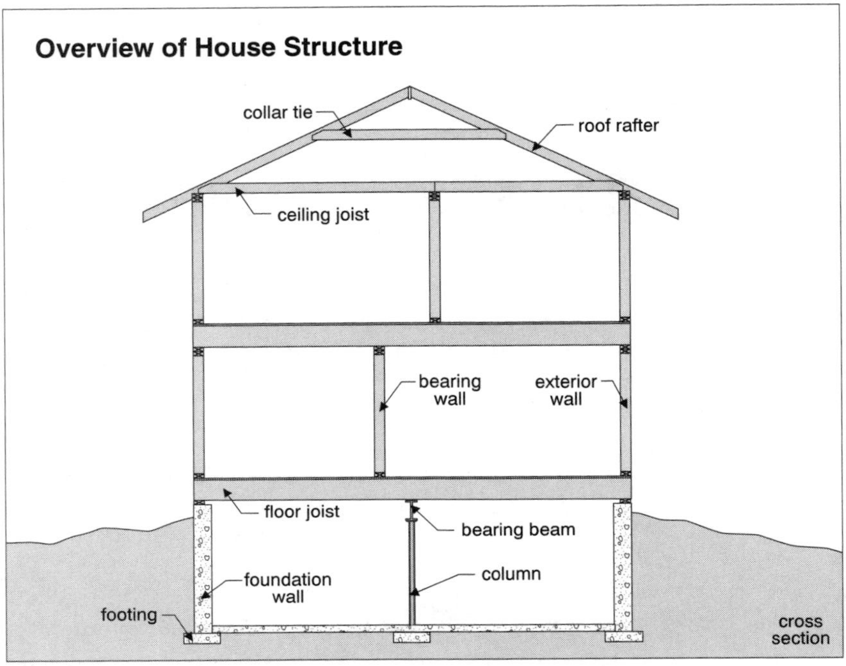

Sometimes, because of soil conditions or an improperly sized footing, the soil under the footing compresses, resulting in a sinking footing. When this happens, a section of the building will settle or sink more rapidly than the rest of the house (see Figure 2.2). This will result in cracks in the basement walls that can extend all the way up the exterior walls of the house. This is a very serious problem that may be expensive or impossible to solve.

The Foundation Walls

The foundation walls are usually made of stone, brick, concrete block, or poured concrete. If the basement is unfinished, you will be able to check the walls for cracks. Moisture penetration, which is also obvious, will be discussed later in Chapter 6.

Different types of cracks occur in foundations. Some of them are serious while others are not. Look for cracks that display significant differential movement. Hairline cracks are not important, but larger cracks (one-quarter of an inch or more) should be studied carefully. It is impor-

FIGURE 2.2 *Types of Settlement*

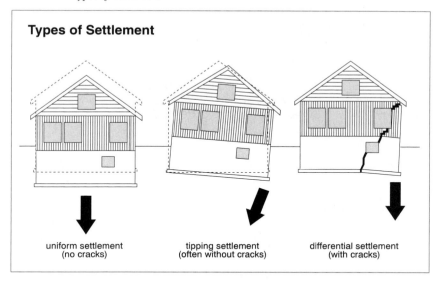

Types of Settlement

| uniform settlement (no cracks) | tipping settlement (often without cracks) | differential settlement (with cracks) |

tant to note the direction of movement, whether it is in one, two, or three planes. Usually, the more planes of movement, the more serious the crack. It is also important to try to determine whether the movement has stopped or is continuing. On older buildings, this is easier because there are more clues. A crack sometimes shows a history of repeated patching, repeated painting, etc. If the paint is old and has not cracked, then odds are that the movement has stopped.

Any significant crack noted in the basement should be followed up through the house and should be viewed from the exterior as well.

The Exterior Walls

Sitting on the foundation walls are the exterior walls of the house. They are usually wood frame with some type of exterior siding or solid masonry. Solid masonry walls (as shown in Figure 2.3) are typically two bricks thick. Usually the two layers are tied together by laying bricks "sideways" so that they interlock the inner and outer layers. This appears as a regular pattern in every sixth or seventh row of bricks. When looking at the outside wall, these rows appear to have short bricks because all that is visible is the end of the brick. Another way to connect two layers of bricks is by using mechanical fasteners. This is not common, though, and almost impossible to detect by visual examination.

FIGURE 2.3 *Solid Masonry Walls*

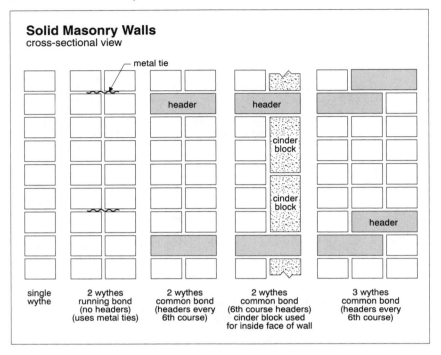

Wood-frame walls usually consist of 2-by-4 vertical members called studs, which are placed 16 inches apart. In older housing, a framing technique known as balloon framing was used. In balloon framing, the floors of the house were hung from the studs, which were continuous from the foundations up to the roof. Platform framing, used more commonly today, is different because each floor level is built as a platform, then the walls are built and erected in sections, resting on the platform. After the walls are constructed, another platform for the next floor is built and the process repeats itself. There are pros and cons to both methods, but neither is considered far superior.

The outside of the studs is sheathed with one of several materials and then the exterior siding is installed. Brick veneer (see Figure 2.4) is real brick; however, only one layer of brick, which is not a structural component, is fastened to the framing with metal ties that are not visible. As a result, there are no rows of short bricks (bricks turned sideways) in the wall. Usually, there is a space between the brick veneer and the sheathing. The mortar is left out of the vertical spaces between every

FIGURE 2.4 *Brick Veneer Wall*

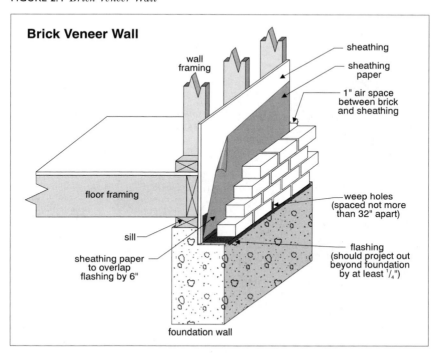

fourth brick at the bottom of the wall to allow any moisture that may accumulate between the brick and the sheathing to drain. Sometimes wicks (short pieces of rope) are installed to draw water out of this cavity.

Inspection

When viewing the exterior wall of a house, it is important to look for movement. This movement may manifest itself in cracks (see Figure 2.5), bowing walls, or walls out of plumb or out of square. Look at walls from various angles. Scan walls, following mortar joints or any other horizontal line that can be picked up, to look for unusual movement.

If walls are sinking or moving, this is a serious structural problem, which sometimes can be corrected by underpinning foundations; however, this is a very expensive proposition. If you suspect serious structural problems with the footings, foundations, or exterior wall systems, and are still interested in the house, it is best to call in an expert.

FIGURE 2.5 *Analyzing Crack Size*

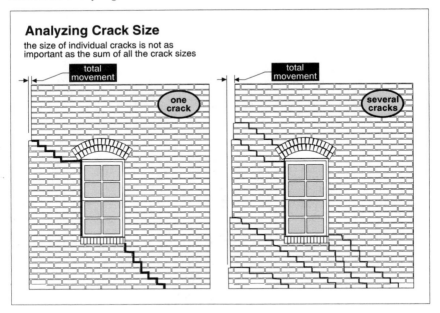

THE INTERNAL STRUCTURE

Besides the perimeter or external structural components, there are internal components as well. The main components, which when joined together and covered to create a floor, are joists. Joists are horizontal wood members, very often spruce. The first floor joists usually sit on the foundation wall and span the width of the house. Joists are usually placed 16 inches apart center to center and, at that spacing, various sizes of spruce joists can span various distances. The following are rules of thumb: 2-by-8s can span 12 feet; 2-by-10s can run 15 feet, 6 inches; and 2-by-12s can bridge an 18-foot, 6-inch distance.

Therefore, if the house is 18 feet wide, the floor joists in the basement may span from one exterior wall to the other. If they are spruce 2-by-12s spaced 16 inches on center, this is adequate. If the house is 24 feet across, the floor joists will probably be 2-by-8s; however, there will be a center wall (masonry or wood frame) or a beam supported with columns so that the spans are reduced to 12 feet. The walls or columns that support the beam must also have footings, but, as with the other footings, they are usually not visible for they are below the floor.

FIGURE 2.6 *Common Causes of Cracked Joists*

Common Causes of Cracked Joists

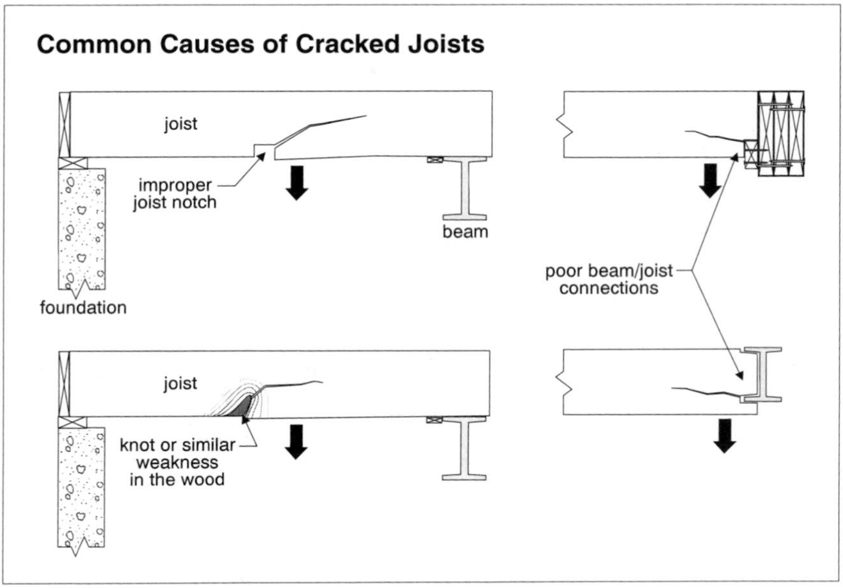

It is important to check joist spans and spacing to determine their suitability (see Figure 2.6). If joists are overspanned, floors are liable to be springy and, with time, quite likely to sag in the center. If the house is older, keep in mind that the house has stood the test of time. If floors have not sagged in 50 years, regardless of joist spans, it is unlikely that they are going to begin to sag now unless something has changed.

While on this point, it should be mentioned that this test of time holds true for most structural components of a house. Many old designs and techniques are considered unorthodox today; however, if there has been no movement of a component in 50 years, and nothing has changed, it is unlikely that there will be any future movement.

After looking at the joists, look at the center beam and columns. Because of various house designs, some houses have none while other houses have one, two, or three beams. Check for sagging of beams between the columns and for column movement. The beams can be wood or steel. Columns can be wood, steel, brick, concrete block, or poured concrete.

Look for structural supports that have been added since the original construction. If there are any, further investigation will be necessary. They may have been installed only to compensate for a heavy piece of furniture or a rattling china cabinet, or there may have been an attempt to rectify a serious structural problem.

Besides properly sizing the wooden structural components, it is necessary to determine whether their structural integrity has been violated by rot or insect attack.

Rot

Rot is a fungus that attacks wood. The term *dry rot* is misleading, for all rot needs moisture to grow. While investigating the basement, look for damp areas or areas that have been damp for reasonably long periods of time. Check the wood members in these areas very closely. Take along an ice pick, or another sharp object, so that any wood that is suspect can be probed to determine the extent of damage.

Termites

Of all the wood-boring insects, none does more damage than termites. Rather than just living in the wood as most wood-boring insects do, termites actually eat wood. Subterranean termites build nests in the soil, which provides a constant source of moisture for them. Because their skin is very thin, they dehydrate very quickly if exposed to the elements. Therefore, subterranean termites live in a protected environment and do not expose themselves to the drying effects of the air. To cross sections of concrete or steel in search of wood, termites build "shelter tubes." Initial tubes are usually small, only about one-quarter of an inch wide, and are constructed of sand and soil cemented together with secretions from the termites. The presence of these tubes usually is the first evidence of termite infestation. Dampwood and drywood termites do not need these shelter tubes and can be more difficult to find. Once inside a piece of wood, subterranean termites tend to eat with the grain. The galleries that they create contain specks of excrement and earth called *frass*. These galleries, parallel to the grain, and the frass inside, help to recognize termite damage. Termites seldom eat through the outer edges of the lumber, so it is important to probe the wood with a sharp object.

Because most termites prefer damp or rotted wood, search for termites and rot in the same area. Termites also tend to enter houses through wood in direct contact with the soil. The bottom of basement stairs and wooden posts in the basement are prime areas for entry. Some old houses are built on wood piers or with sill plates directly in contact with the soil. These conditions are most common in houses with crawl spaces.

To remove subterranean termites from a house requires chemical treatment. Chemicals are injected into the soil through the basement walls and floors to provide a chemical barrier. The treatment typically lasts 10 to 25 years, depending on the pesticide used. In row housing, it is important to treat the entire building to prevent the entry of termites from next door. It is also necessary to break all wood/soil contact in the house. In some cases, this is a minor job, but in others this means resupporting the entire structure—a very costly undertaking. Dampwood and drywood termite infestations are generally treated by tenting and fumigating the house.

If termites are discovered in the house you are inspecting, it is not necessarily the end of the world. If caught early on, termites can be effectively stopped without doing much damage. On the other hand, advanced termite attack can virtually destroy a house.

While other wood-boring insects can damage a house, few can cause as much damage as termites. However, in your inspection, evidence of damage by carpenter ants, powder post beetles, wharf borers, and weevils should be noted.

SUMMARY

The single most serious problem in a house is the failure of footings and/or foundations. If the building is settling, corrective action can be prohibitively expensive. If the movement has stopped, no repairs may be necessary unless perfectly level floors are important.

Sagging floor joists generally do not indicate major difficulties and repairs often are optional. Replacing individual damaged components such as a joist, beam, or column is often less expensive than most people expect.

Termites and rot can do serious structural damage. However, the early stages of attack can be readily detected, and corrective action taken, usually at moderate cost. If the damage is extensive, consider getting some professional advice.

CHECKLIST—The Structure

1. Foundation wall cracks?

2. Interior or exterior wall cracking?

3. Active movement?

4. Joist size adequate?

5. Beams and columns adequate?

6. Rot or termite damage?

7. Sloping floors?

8. Sagging floors?

9. Walls out of plumb?

10. Doorjambs out of square?

3

THE ELECTRICAL SERVICE

The electrical service in a house is typically one of the least understood and most often abused systems. Electrical faults cause a tremendous number of home fires every year. Furthermore, inadequate electrical service is a major inconvenience and detracts from the overall comfort and usability of a home.

Electricity can be looked at in two segments. First, consider the amount of power coming into a home. This is called the size, capacity, or amperage of the service. Second, the bulk electricity brought into the house must be distributed to end-use areas throughout the house. This is accomplished by using branch circuits of various sizes.

It may be helpful to think of electricity as behaving much like water. The amount of water available from a faucet depends on the size of the pipe feeding the faucet. It also depends on the amount of pressure pushing the water through the piping. In an electrical system, the size of the wire can be thought of as the size of the pipe. The diameter of the wire determines the capacity of the wire. The pressure forcing the water through pipes is measured in pounds per square inch. In electricity, the pressure is measured in volts. The amount of water that passes through a pipe is considered in terms of gallons per minute. With electricity, this is analogous to amperes or amps (current).

FIGURE 3.1 *120/240 Volts*

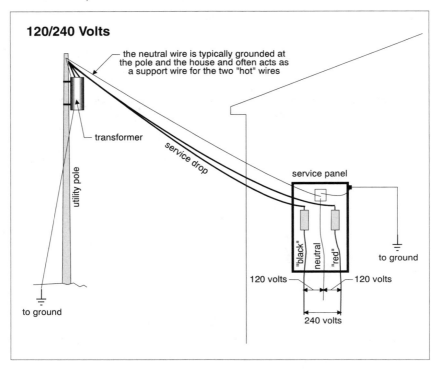

Electricity for a house is supplied from the electric cables in the street. In older neighborhoods, these wires are run overhead on poles, while in newer neighborhoods the wires may be run underground. Electricity for a house is obtained by tapping into these wires and running either an overhead or underground line into the house. Typically, three wires are run, providing 240-volt service (see Figure 3.1). If only two wires are provided, this usually indicates 120-volt service. Old 120-volt services are generally considered inadequate and unsafe for most modern lifestyles. Most houses are provided with a nominal 240-volt service and, apart from minor fluctuations, there is very little choice in the amount of electrical pressure available.

The overhead cables should not be located close to tree branches and should not be easily reached from porches, balconies, or decks.

THE SIZE OF THE SERVICE

The electrical capacity of any house is determined by the size of the conductors leading from the street into the building. Because of the various types of cable and the different thicknesses of insulation, it is difficult to visually judge the ampacity of the incoming wire. Later we will talk more about how we can determine the size of the electrical service. First, let's look at the common ones.

The *30-amp service* still exists in some older homes. This is generally considered unacceptable and, while a few homes do operate satisfactorily with this, some lifestyle compromises are required.

The *60-amp electrical service* is commonly found in houses built before 1960. This service is of marginal capacity for most modern households. Depending on the size of house and the electrical load, a 60-amp service may prove adequate. Where major appliances are electrically powered, however, this service is often inadequate. For example, if the stove, water heater, and clothes dryer are all electric, the load introduced by these major appliances and the ordinary household appliances may overtax the 60-amp service. If electric central air-conditioning is added, 100-amp service will almost certainly be required. The number of people and rooms in a house also affect the electrical demand. A general recommendation with regard to a house with 60-amp service is to live with it for a few months to determine your specific requirements. If the service is inadequate, convert to 100-amp service. In some areas, insurance companies consider 60-amp services as old and undersized. These insurers may not offer coverage on homes with 60-amp services, or they may charge higher premiums.

The *100-amp service* is provided in most modern homes and provides adequate power for most average-size (three-bedroom) dwellings. One exception would be an electrically heated house (which requires greater supply). Multifamily dwellings, of course, require special consideration.

The *200-amp service* is used in large single-family residences and small, multifamily dwellings. Also, houses that are electrically heated very often are provided with 100-amp electrical supply for the heating system and 100-amps for the normal household requirements.

In various areas, intermediate size services are provided. For example, 70-amp, 125-amp, and 150-amp services are installed. If it is neces-

FIGURE 3.2 *Determining Service Size by the Service Entrance Wires*

Determining Service Size by the Service Entrance Wires

check the size of the service entrance conductors at the masthead or inside the service box

service entrance conductors

service entrance conductors

service mast

to ground

drip loop

service box

to distribution panel

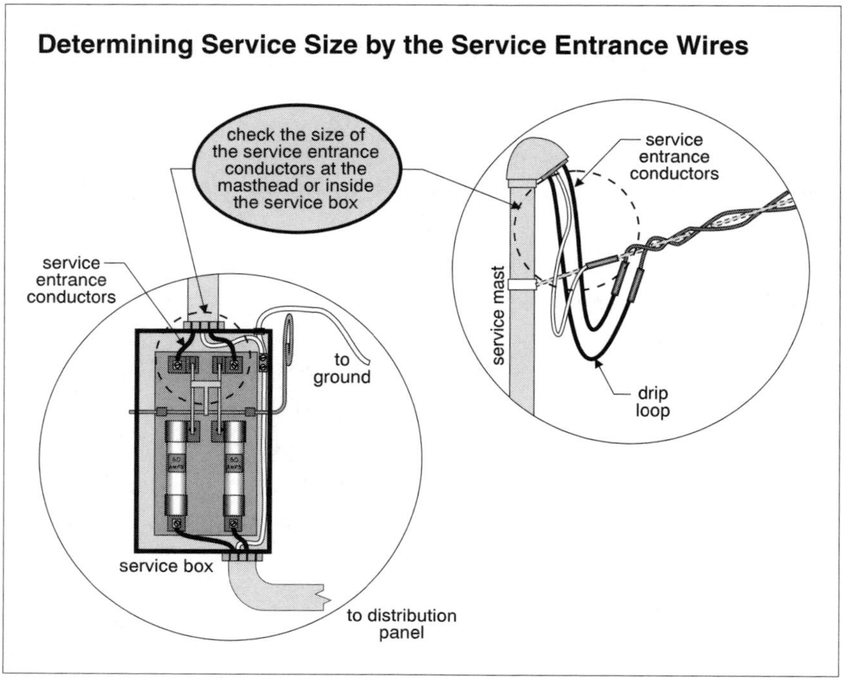

sary to upgrade the electrical service, the expense is less than most people anticipate. Remember, this involves changing only the wire from the street to the house. One exception is where underground service into the house is provided and the conduit enclosing the cables is so small that larger cables cannot be introduced. The existing conduit must be excavated and replaced with a larger one. In any case, upgrading the size of the electrical service involves no changes to the wiring that distributes electricity within the house.

HOW TO DETERMINE SERVICE SIZE

As discussed, the amount of electricity is determined by the size of the service entrance cables (see Figure 3.2). Also, it is very difficult to tell how big these wires are simply by looking at them. As soon as these wires enter the house, they must pass through a main disconnect switch, which is provided with fuses or a circuit breaker. With few exceptions,

FIGURE 3.3 *Determining Service Size by the Main Disconnect*

Determining Service Size by the Main Disconnect

check the amperage rating of the main breaker

check the amperage rating of the main fuses

to ground

note:
the panel (box) rating should be no smaller than the fuses/breakers

service box

combination panel

to distribution panel

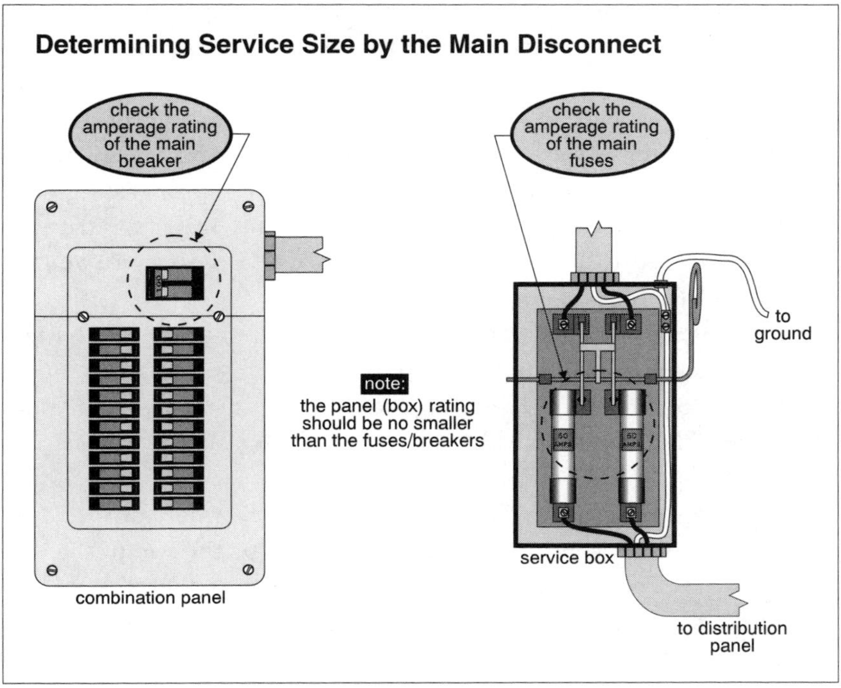

the size of the fuses or circuit breaker can be determined readily, and this should indicate the size of the electrical service (see Figure 3.3).

Where two cartridge-type fuses are provided in one disconnect switch, the size (number of amps) written on each fuse should be the same. This number indicates the electrical service capacity. Thus, two 100-amp fuses represent 100-amp service. Two 60-amp fuses represent 60-amp service. This is the best way to determine the size of the incoming service. However, one point is stressed: The fuses are not usually visible without opening a cover panel. This cover panel may be sealed by the local utility and, if this is the case, the seal should not be broken. If the panel can be opened, do this with the greatest caution. Regardless of whether the main disconnect switch is on or off, there is enough electricity in this box to kill. *Nothing within the box should be touched.* Someone experienced should do this, such as an electrician.

Where the main disconnect is a circuit breaker, the size is written or stamped on the breaker handle itself and it is not necessary to open the panel to check the size.

A number of fallacies exist about how the size of an electrical service can be determined. Many people say that the rating stamped on the front of the disconnect or distribution of boxes will indicate the size of the service. This is not the case! These readings indicate the maximum allowable service entering these boxes and are restrictions imposed by the manufacturer of the boxes. Sometimes it is said that adding up the number of fuses and multiplying by 15, or adding up the rating of all the fuses, will indicate the electrical service. Again, this is not true and there is no fixed relationship between the size of the service and the number or size of the fuses.

The rating on the electric meter is simply a maximum allowable determined by the meter manufacturer. In some cases, 100-amp meters are located on houses with 200-amp service. At times, it is maintained that where the meter is on the outside of the house, the service is at least 100-amps. Again, this is not the case.

The size of the electrical conduit running down the outside of the house is occasionally used as a measuring stick for the size of the electrical service. This, too, is an inconclusive measure of the capacity. The size of the conduit usually reflects only the size of the conduit the electrician had at the time of installation. Many cases are found where large conduits capable of carrying 200-amp wires are, in fact, housing wires suitable for only 60-amps.

One other misconception is that if the electrical service panel is at the front of the house, it has been upgraded to at least 100-amps. Again, this is not a reliable indicator.

Following are the cable sizes commonly used with the basic 30-, 60-, 100-, and 200-amp services. Where the size of the cable can be determined from the printing on the sheathing, this will determine what type of electrical service is provided.

Service Size	Conductor Size (United States)		Conductor Size (Canada)	
	Copper	Aluminum	Copper	Aluminum
For 30-amp service	#10	#8	#10	#8
For 60-amp service	# 6	#6	# 6	#6
For 100-amp service	# 4	#2	# 3	#2
For 200-amp service	#00 or 2/0	#0000 or 4/0	#000 or 3/0	250MCM

FIGURE 3.4 *Grounding Equipment*

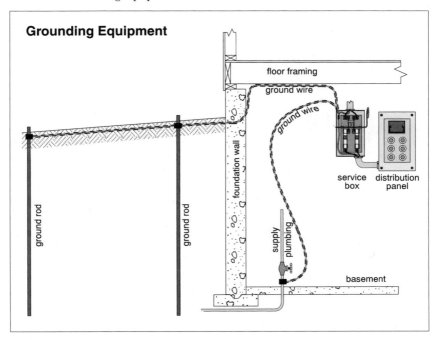

Grounding Equipment

From this chart it can be seen that copper and aluminum wires of different sizes are capable of carrying the same amount of electricity. This is because copper is a better electrical conductor.

One last note: Although the main service entrance cables and associated fuses or circuit breakers are installed by an electrician, in some cases the fuse sizing may be inappropriate. Where this is the case, one will get a false reading of the actual electrical capacity of the system. It is very difficult for anyone but an electrical contractor or inspector to determine this.

GROUNDING

The electrical system should be grounded, using a wire connected either to the plumbing system or to ground rods (as shown in Figure 3.4). This grounding wire provides an emergency path for electricity in the case of a malfunction of an electrical appliance or a short circuit. The ground wire provides an easy route for electricity to take. With a properly grounded system, the electricity will be led harmlessly to the earth.

Look for a wire that leads from the main disconnect switch to the plumbing system or rods sunk into the ground. The following chart shows the size of copper ground wire required for various service sizes. Aluminum ground wires should be one size larger.

Wire Gauge	Service Size (USA)
#8	Up to 125 amp
#6	Up to 175 amp
#4	Up to 200 amp

In the United States, if the connection is to a ground rod, 6-gauge wire is the largest size required.

In some cases, plumbing has been changed and the grounding wire has not been reconnected. If there is a water meter on the system, the ground wire must be connected on the street side of the water meter or a jumper wire must bypass the meter providing a continuous electrical path to ground.

In houses that do not have a municipal water supply system, the supply piping cannot be used as a grounding vehicle.

DISTRIBUTION THROUGHOUT THE HOUSE

Once electricity is available inside the house, it is distributed through a number of branch circuits to areas where it will be used. One reason the electricity is broken up into small branch circuits is that if there is a malfunction and subsequent blowing of a fuse or tripping of a circuit breaker, all electric power and lighting will not be lost in the house. Also, the smaller wiring required in branch circuits is less expensive and easier to work with than are the larger cables. Minimum requirements for most modern houses include two 240-volt circuits and sixteen 120-volt circuits. (Most light fixtures and electrical outlets will be 120-volt, while heavy-duty appliances such as stoves, clothes dryers, water heaters, and central air-conditioning systems will be 240-volt.)

Each 120-volt circuit typically uses a 14-gauge copper wire that is protected by a 15-amp circuit breaker or fuse. The 240-volt circuits employ larger wires that are protected by larger fuses or breakers.

FIGURE 3.5 *Fuse Types*

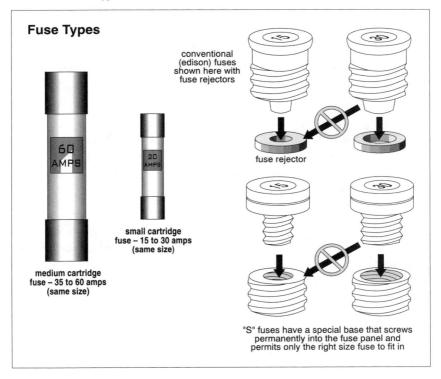

Fuses and circuit breakers are necessary because wire has no means of protecting itself from overheating when too much current is allowed to pass through. This is unlike a water pipe, which can restrict the flow through the pipe by the frictional forces that offer resistance. An electrical appliance that is operating satisfactorily has enough resistance to electrical flow to prevent the wire from overheating. When the appliance malfunctions, or short circuits, however, that resistance is lost and a tremendous amount of electricity is allowed to pass through the wire. This will lead to overheating, melting insulation, sparks, and eventually a fire. A fuse or circuit breaker acts as a safety valve that shuts off the circuit when too much electricity is passed through. The fuse or breaker may be considered the brain of the electrical system, causing an emergency shutdown.

A fuse is a one-time safety device that must be replaced once it has blown. A circuit breaker is a switching device that can be reset subsequent to being tripped. Consequently, circuit breakers are considered more convenient. Furthermore, because circuit breakers are not often replaced by the homeowner, there is less chance that an incorrectly sized breaker will be installed. Unfortunately, the insulated, cylindrical glass, screw-in fuses are physically interchangeable over a 15- to 30-amp size range (see Figure 3.5). Thus, it is very easy for someone to replace a blown 15-amp fuse with a 30-amp fuse. As discussed, this will not provide overcurrent protection for the standard 14-gauge wire.

Safety devices that can prevent overfusing are known as *fuse adapters* or *fuse rejectors*. When placed in a fuse block, they limit the size of the fuse that can be screwed in. Certain adapters allow no more than 15-amp fuses and others allow nothing larger than 20-amp fuses.

Some people maintain that circuit breakers are not as safe as fuses for a breaker switch can become stuck in the open position. This can be overcome by operating the breakers manually from time to time. A monthly checking routine is often recommended. Fuses, too, may have manufacturing defects by which a fuse rated at 15 amps will, in fact, not blow at the designed rate of current flow. Because a fuse is a one-time device, each fuse cannot be tested as it is produced without destroying it. According to most people, the convenience and safety of circuit breakers make them a more desirable alternative.

CHECKING THE FUSE BOX OR CIRCUIT BREAKER PANEL

If you have a fuse box, look at the number of fuses in the panel and note their size (see Figure 3.6). This is clearly marked on the fuse. If the house has an electric stove and an electric clothes dryer, there will be two sets of large fuses. These fuses are usually not the screw-in type and are referred to as cartridge fuses. A stove would typically use 2, 40-amp cartridge-type fuses and a clothes dryer 2, 30-amp fuses. There may be as few as 2, 15-amp fuses and as many as 40 or 50. However, 16 is a common number and the minimum acceptable for an average-size (three-bedroom) house. Sometimes fuses will be provided, but not connected. In other cases, there is room in the panel for additional fuses (and, therefore, more circuits).

If your house has a circuit breaker panel instead of a fuse box, check the number of switches (breakers) and the amperage marked on them. As discussed previously, if the house has an electric stove and electric

FIGURE 3.6 *Typical Arrangement of Panel Wires*

Typical Arrangement of Panel Wires

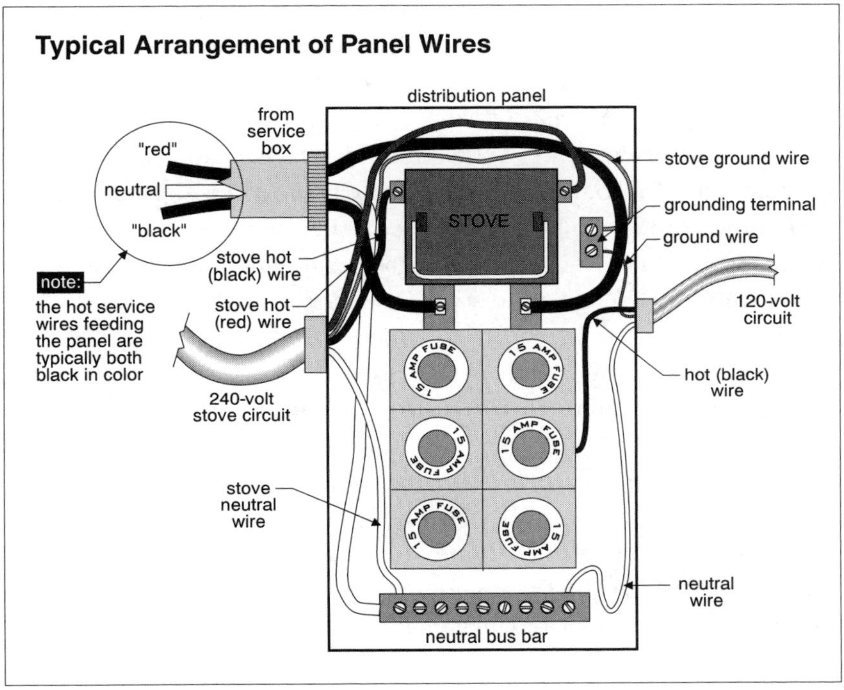

clothes dryer, there should be 2 switches marked 40 amp and 2 marked 30 amp. There should also be at least 16 switches labeled 15 amp.

A complete electrical investigation involves removing the cover on the fuse box or circuit breaker panel. Unless you are familiar with electricity, however, don't do this yourself because all wiring within the box is live. If the cover is removed, though, it is possible to compare the size of the wire to the size of the fuse or circuit breaker protecting it. The chart that follows indicates proper protection for various sizes and types of wire.

	Wire Gauge	
Fuse or Breaker Rating	**Copper**	**Aluminum**
For 15-amp fuses	#14	#12
For 20-amp fuses	#12	#10
For 25-amp fuses	#10	#10
For 30-amp fuses	#10	# 8
For 40-amp fuses	# 8	# 6

If you are inspecting this yourself, make sure that all fuses or breakers are properly sized. Sometimes it is difficult to determine the size of the wiring. Often it is written on the sheathing on the cable, which can be read outside the fuse box or panel. It may also be helpful to carry a sample length of each size of wire for comparison.

Look for evidence of overheating, burned insulation, or arcing. A humming noise or burned insulation smell are danger signs that should be followed up by a qualified electrician. Loose connections and wires not secured to a terminal also indicate problems. Rust in the box or panel should be further investigated and the source of the moisture eliminated.

Note whether all of the fuse or breaker terminals are occupied. If there is room for more circuits, this will reduce the cost of expanding the system.

When the cover is replaced, there should be no open holes that allow contact with live components. Circuits that are not in use should be filled with fuses or covers designed for this use. Check the point where the cables pass through the wall of the distribution box where there are often signs of mechanical damage to the cables.

WIRING THROUGHOUT THE HOUSE

The electrical cables running from the box may be in rigid metal conduits, flexible metal conduits, or nonmetallic sheathed cable. The nonmetallic sheathing may be cloth, paper, or plastic. Most modern cables contain a black and a white conductor (see Figure 3.7), each provided with its own insulation within the cable. There is also a ground wire, which is typically uninsulated. The black and white wires, when connected to electrical fixtures, complete the circuit. The ground wire, as discussed previously, provides an emergency safety route for the electricity. Some of the older cable, which contains a black and a white conductor, will not have a ground wire. In this case, individual receptacles will not be grounded.

The oldest wire used residentially is commonly referred to as *knob-and-tube*. It is readily identified by the white ceramic insulators that support the wire where it changes direction (knobs) and passes through wood members (tubes) as shown in Figure 3.8. With this type, the two wires run separately, usually insulated with cloth. This wiring has not

FIGURE 3.7 *Number of Conductors*

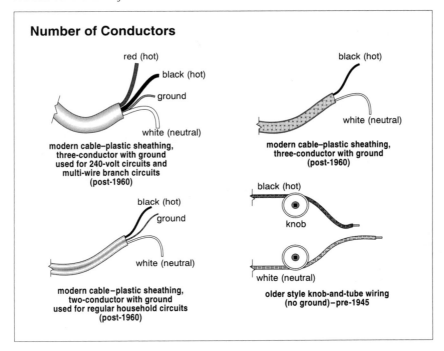

Number of Conductors

red (hot)

black (hot)

ground

white (neutral)

modern cable–plastic sheathing,
three-conductor with ground
used for 240-volt circuits and
multi-wire branch circuits
(post-1960)

black (hot)

ground

white (neutral)

modern cable–plastic sheathing,
two-conductor with ground
used for regular household circuits
(post-1960)

black (hot)

white (neutral)

modern cable–plastic sheathing,
three-conductor with ground
(post-1960)

black (hot)

knob

white (neutral)

older style knob-and-tube wiring
(no ground)–pre-1945

been used extensively since about 1950. Unless the wiring has been mechanically damaged, tapped into amateurishly, or overfused, however, it is often completely serviceable. Evidence of mechanical abuse is worn off or broken insulation and household items leaning against or hanging from the wires.

Original connections on this type of wire were covered with cloth electrical tape. Where modern two-conductor cable has been connected to it, a closed metal junction box should be provided.

Past overfusing can be detected by flexing the wire slightly because overfusing can cause the cable to become brittle. With a little experience, one can determine what is normal flexibility. Again, a note of caution: *Power supply should be shut off before flexing the knob-and-tube wires to avoid the potential for electric shock.* Often a house has been rewired, in part, and the wiring is a combination of modern two-conductor cables and older knob-and-tube wiring. This is not necessarily a bad situation. However, one must look carefully to see which wire is in service. Very often the old knob-and-tube wiring is left in place, although it is no longer functional.

FIGURE 3.8 *Knob-and-Tube Wiring*

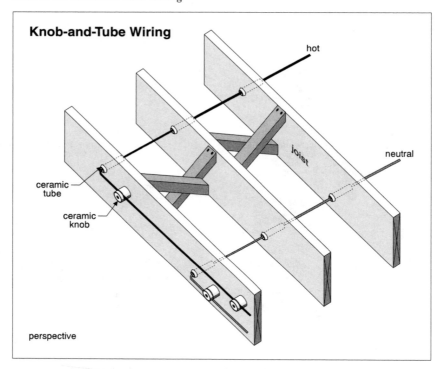

As with 60-amp services, many insurance companies are reluctant to insure homes with old knob-and-tube wiring and will charge higher premiums, if they will insure the home at all.

Regardless of its type, wiring should be well supported at regular intervals. It is better to run the wiring through holes drilled in the joists rather than on the joist surfaces. Sometimes when cable is pulled through holes in wood members, however, the insulation can be damaged. Look for evidence of this. Wiring should not be run on exposed wall, floor, or ceiling surfaces and, generally speaking, should be protected from mechanical damage, within practical limits.

Check the quality of connections at wire junctions and at fixtures; a metal junction box should be provided. In many cases, covers are left off boxes or connections are made without a box. An old light fixture with the lightbulb itself supported by the electric wiring is not considered sound and should be replaced.

As you walk through the house, note the number of electrical outlets in each room and in the hallways. In modern homes an outlet is

FIGURE 3.9 *Ground Fault Interrupter*

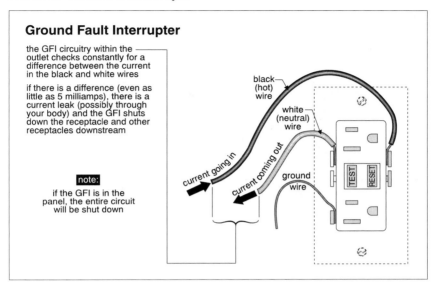

Ground Fault Interrupter

the GFI circuitry within the outlet checks constantly for a difference between the current in the black and white wires

if there is a difference (even as little as 5 milliamps), there is a current leak (possibly through your body) and the GFI shuts down the receptacle and other receptacles downstream

note:
if the GFI is in the panel, the entire circuit will be shut down

black (hot) wire

white (neutral) wire

current going in
current coming out

ground wire

TEST   RESET

provided for every 12 feet of wall space in most rooms. That means, a 10-by-12-foot room should have approximately 4 receptacles. There is usually 1 outlet for every 15 feet of hallway. A person should not have to reach more than 3 feet horizontally along the kitchen counter to find an outlet. There should be at least 1 outlet in every bathroom, located as far away from the bathtub or shower as is practical. Most modern houses also have at least 1 outdoor electrical receptacle.

If you have an electric stove or clothes dryer, check whether wiring has been provided for these appliances. Because many houses have gas stoves and clothes dryers, heavy-duty electrical circuits will have to be added.

Older houses will not have the full complement of electric supply; however, wholesale upgrading is often unnecessary. Where there are few outlets, it may be necessary to add one in each room. Generally, you should live in a house for a number of months before deciding exactly where to add electrical outlets.

A representative sample of electrical outlets can be tested using a circuit analyzer or tester. These inexpensive devices are available in most hardware stores. The tester will indicate whether an outlet is powered and whether it is wired correctly.

FIGURE 3.10 *Stairway Lighting*

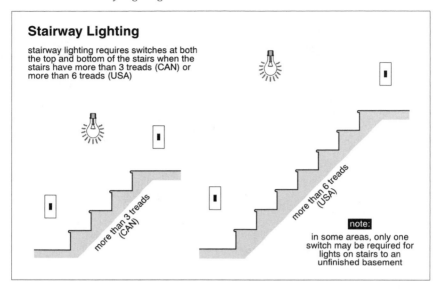

On new installations, electrical outlets in bathrooms, on exterior walls, and sometimes in kitchens should be Ground Fault Interrupting type units (see Figure 3.9). These special outlets provide very sensitive overcurrent protection devices. In the event of even a minor ground fault, the unit will trip. This type of installation is readily identified by a test button on the outlet itself or on the circuit breaker at the panel.

Most older electrical outlets have two slots to receive standard two-prong electrical plugs. Modern electrical receptacles have a third U-shaped slot to receive the grounding plug found on some modern appliances. This third slot should be connected to a ground wire, provided in the cable, which eventually is grounded at the plumbing system as described previously. The circuit tester will tell you whether or not the ground protection has, in fact, been provided. The U-ground receptacles do provide additional protection only when a three-prong plug is connected to it. Most typical electrical appliances have only two prongs and no grounding protection is afforded. Thus, replacement of the two-prong receptacles and ungrounded cable is often not cost-effective. Adding new U-ground receptacles connected to the older ungrounded cable provides no additional protection. This arrangement may lead to a false sense of security. A ground wire is not necessary if the appliances are *double insulated.* These appliances, even when used with a two-prong system, will be safe.

Notice the number and location of light fixtures and switches. Many old houses have few overhead lights. Lighting for stairwells should be operable from switches at the top and bottom of the stairwell (see Figure 3.10). Lighting around the furnace and other service areas in the basement is a must. Lighting in clothes closets usually indicates a high-quality home.

Where wiring is run on the building exterior (e.g., to a porch light), the wire should be enclosed in a waterproof conduit or should be specifically approved for outdoor use.

ALUMINUM WIRING

Most house wiring is copper, although aluminum was used extensively in some parts of the country from the mid-1960s through the mid-1970s. Initially, aluminum wiring was considered desirable because of its low cost. Aluminum wire is not as good an electrical conductor as copper, but this was recognized initially and larger wire was used.

Some problems with aluminum have since been identified. Because aluminum is very soft, electricians must take greater care when working with it than with copper. Aluminum has a higher coefficient of thermal expansion than copper does. This means that when the aluminum wire heats up as current passes through, it tends to expand more than a copper wire will. Correspondingly, when the wire cools off, it shrinks more than copper does. The result is movement of the wire at its terminal connections. Aluminum wiring is said to "creep" out from under a terminal screw connection because of this repeated expansion and contraction.

All metals oxidize or rust to some degree. Fortunately, the oxide that forms on copper is electrically conductive and no problems are presented. Less fortunately, the oxides of aluminum are poor electrical conductors and resistance to electrical flow can be caused by a coating of oxide on the aluminum. Incidentally, the oxide on aluminum is not red, but a whitish color. The oxide found on copper is green.

The oxide forms on an aluminum surface that is exposed to the air. The combination of the poor electrical conductivity of the aluminum oxide and the fact that new metal is regularly exposed by the expansion and contraction can lead to high resistance and overheating at electrical terminals.

FIGURE 3.11 *CUAL Designation*

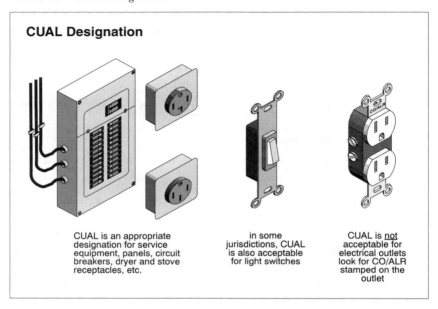

CUAL Designation

CUAL is an appropriate designation for service equipment, panels, circuit breakers, dryer and stove receptacles, etc.

in some jurisdictions, CUAL is also acceptable for light switches

CUAL is not acceptable for electrical outlets look for CO/ALR stamped on the outlet

When aluminum wiring was initially introduced, some of these problems were not recognized. Within a few years, concern was expressed and electrical connectors were redesigned. Special connectors designated CUAL (see Figure 3.11) were manufactured for such things as distribution panels, circuit breaker blocks, fuse blocks, wire nuts, and electrical receptacles. The improvements worked well in all areas except for the electrical receptacles. Further revision was made to the outlets and the designation was changed to CO/ALR. This revision proved satisfactory. When aluminum wiring is found, look for these special outlets. In some areas, switches must also be CO/ALR. One other solution that works for retrofit in some cases is to connect a short length of copper wire to the aluminum and then secure the copper wire to a standard receptacle. The copper/aluminum connection should be made with an appropriately designated CUAL connector or a proprietary system called Copalum. Different jurisdictions allow different methods, so find out what is accepted in your area.

Aluminum wire can usually be spotted by reading the information on the outside of the cable. The word *Aluminum* or *Alum* will be indicated somewhere. If the cable is not visible, you can check by removing the cover plate from an electrical outlet. If an aluminum conductor is noted, remember to look on the front of the outlet for the CO/ALR designation.

SUMMARY

The electrical system is one of the most important in a house because of the hazards posed by faulty wiring. Upgrading the capacity of the service involves working outside the house for the most part. Upgrading is not considered a major expense (usually it costs less than $1,500 for a 100-amp service). Rewiring an entire house is expensive, but rarely necessary. If a house is to be gutted and renovated, rewiring is relatively easy. Where the electrician has to work around wall and ceiling finishes, the cost increases significantly. Adding circuits and/or receptacles and making minor repairs are small jobs from a cost standpoint, but important where safety may be compromised. The presence of aluminum wiring need not be a major concern. With good installation and the proper connectors, there should be no problem. Providing the proper connectors on a retrofit basis is not usually a major expense.

CHECKLIST—The Electrical Service

1. Size of service?

2. Proper grounding?

3. Fuse or circuit breakers?

4. Fuse or circuit breaker sizes?

5. Number of circuits?

6. Distribution wire: old or new?

7. Adequately supported?

8. Open connections?

9. Aluminum wiring?

10. Sufficient number of outlets throughout the house?

11. Overhead light fixtures where necessary?

4

THE PLUMBING

The plumbing system in a house is composed of several components: a water source, distribution piping, a drainage system, venting, fixtures, and, finally, a waste-disposal system.

WATER SOURCE

In urban areas, water is usually supplied by the municipality via water mains in the street. This should be verified, however, for some suburban areas still rely on well water. Rural homes usually rely on wells. There are two different types of wells: deep and shallow. Wells less than 25 feet in depth are considered shallow, while deeper wells can be up to several hundred feet. The depth of the well depends on the water table. Deeper wells tend to be less vulnerable to contamination; however, regardless of the type of well, water samples should be tested by the local health authorities.

Several different types of pumps can be used in conjunction with wells (see Figure 4.1). There are older-style reciprocating or piston pumps, and more modern jet centrifugal pumps and submersible centrifugal pumps. Submersible pumps are located within the well itself

FIGURE 4.1 *Types of Pumps*

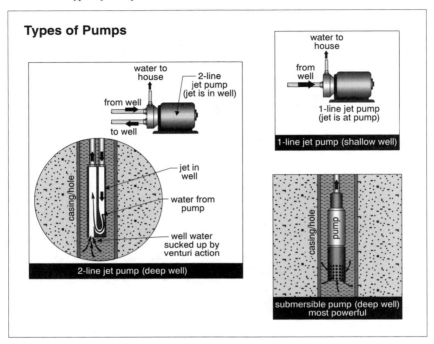

and are typically used in deep wells. Surface pumps can be located at the top of the well in a well house or within the basement area of the house itself. If the pump is outdoors, precautions must be taken to ensure that the pump does not freeze.

In conjunction with the pump is a storage pressure tank (see Figure 4.2). This tank can vary in size from holding just a few gallons to several hundred gallons. The tank serves a dual purpose. It not only stores water, but it acts as a means of providing steady water pressure. Because water is relatively incompressible, a portion of the tank should be filled with air. The air is easily compressible and when there is a demand for water within the house, the air pressure within the storage tank provides the pressure to force the water out. In this manner, the pressure in the tank slowly reduces as the air expands. When the pressure gets to the lower limit of the pressure switch, the pump is reactivated to force more water into the tank, which compresses the air once again. As time passes, the air within the tank gets absorbed into the water and eventually the tank becomes waterlogged. When this happens, the tank

FIGURE 4.2 *Pressure Tank Components and Pump Controls*

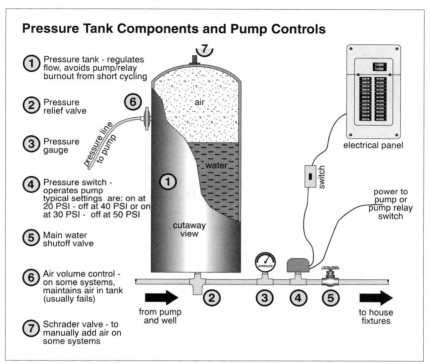

Pressure Tank Components and Pump Controls

① Pressure tank - regulates flow, avoids pump/relay burnout from short cycling

② Pressure relief valve

③ Pressure gauge

④ Pressure switch - operates pump typical settings are: on at 20 PSI - off at 40 PSI or on at 30 PSI - off at 50 PSI

⑤ Main water shutoff valve

⑥ Air volume control - on some systems, maintains air in tank (usually fails)

⑦ Schrader valve - to manually add air on some systems

is full of water. Any demand for water within the house will drop pressure in the tank very quickly and cause the pump to come on and off repeatedly. This is a minor problem that can be rectified by draining water from, and adding more air into, the tank. The pump and tank should be checked for leaks and any obvious signs of deterioration.

If the water supply to the house is provided by the municipality, the pipe feeding water into the building is usually found near the exterior walls in the basement. Typically, it is at the front of the house coming up through the basement floor. Near the point of entry into the house, should be a main shutoff valve and, in some cases, also a water meter (see Figure 4.3). Ideally, the main valve will have a waste, or bleed, valve that can be used to drain the supply plumbing system. Depending on the age of the house, the pipe leading in from the street may be any one of several materials and sizes. In very old homes, the pipe may be made of lead. Lead pipe is easily identified by the large ball type connection at the joints and by its soft grayish color and texture. This pipe can be

FIGURE 4.3 *Main Shutoff Valve–Stop and Waste*

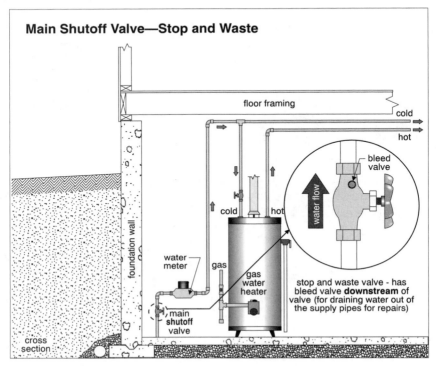

easily scored with a pocketknife, which will expose a shiny surface. If the incoming pipe is lead, the water should be tested by the local authorities for lead content. Galvanized steel and copper are the other most commonly used materials and they will be dealt with further in the distribution section of this chapter.

On newer, average-size (three-bedroom) homes, the incoming pipe is commonly three-quarters of an inch. On older homes, it is usually one-half-inch piping, and on some very old homes, it is three-eighths of an inch. Larger homes sometimes have one-inch and even one-and-one-half-inch supply piping.

Generally, the condition of the pipe up to the property line is the responsibility of the municipality. Beyond the property line, it is the responsibility of the homeowner.

DISTRIBUTION PIPING

Past the shutoff valve and the water meter, the piping starts supplying water to the various fixtures within the house. Usually, the first fixture to be supplied is the water heater. From the water heater, the piping generally runs in tandem (hot- and cold-water pipes) to the various fixtures throughout the house. Typically, the pipes are spaced four to six inches apart to prevent the hot water from warming the cold and vice versa.

The water heater is commonly powered by electricity, natural gas, or oil. In some municipalities, the vast majority of the units are rented from the local electric or gas companies. If this is the case, there is usually a rental sticker on the unit and its condition is not a major concern. A small rental fee is included on your utilities bill.

Water heaters have an average life expectancy of 10 to 12 years. If the unit is not rented, it should be inspected carefully for leakage and rust at the seams and at the piping connections.

Gas- or oil-fired hot water heaters typically have between a 30-gallon and 40-gallon capacity. This size of heater should provide adequate hot water for a family of four. Electrically heated units often have a somewhat larger capacity because of their slower recovery rate.

The supply piping within the house is usually made of galvanized steel, copper, or plastic. Plastic piping is not allowed in many jurisdictions and only allowed on cold-water piping in others. It is sometimes installed without the authorization of the local authorities. If plastic supply piping is encountered, this should be investigated.

Galvanized steel supply piping (see Figure 4.4) has not been installed in houses for the past 40 to 50 years. This piping is easily identified by its threaded joints. Depending on the water used, and the frequency of use, galvanized piping has an average life expectancy of 40 to 50 years, so any that you see will likely be reaching the end of its life. It tends to rust from the inside out. The rust usually starts to appear on the outside of the pipe at the threaded connections where the pipe is thinnest. The internal diameter of the pipe decreases with age as rust and scale build up within the pipe. The hot-water piping tends to deteriorate more quickly than the cold deteriorates because the elevated temperatures accelerate the rusting process. The horizontal sections of pipe, commonly located in the basement, also rust more quickly. This

FIGURE 4.4 *Galvanized Steel Pipe*

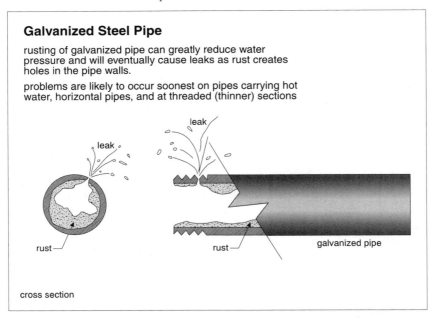

Galvanized Steel Pipe

rusting of galvanized pipe can greatly reduce water pressure and will eventually cause leaks as rust creates holes in the pipe walls.

problems are likely to occur soonest on pipes carrying hot water, horizontal pipes, and at threaded (thinner) sections

reduction in the size of the inner diameter of the pipe results in low water pressure. The pipe eventually rusts through and leaks.

Copper supply piping has a much longer life span. It usually lasts the lifetime of the house. (Certain types of acidic water, however, can deteriorate copper piping at an accelerated rate.) Copper piping can be identified by its soldered joints—there are no threads. Sometimes when supply piping has been painted, it is difficult to ascertain what type of pipe it is. It may be wise to carry a magnet, which will be attracted to the galvanized pipe, but not to copper.

Replacing older galvanized supply piping with copper is very expensive, so try to determine how much galvanized pipe remains. Inspect all visible sections of piping. The largest portions of the pipe can usually be seen in the basement (if it is unfinished). It is very common for homeowners to replace sections of galvanized piping as it wears out. Therefore, if you see some copper piping, do not assume that it is all copper. Each line must be followed. It is not uncommon to see a pipe change from copper to galvanized and back again several times during its run through a house. The horizontal sections of pipe that tend to wear out more quickly are often replaced prior to the vertical runs. This is partially because the horizontal sections are readily accessible in the basement while the vertical sections are usually buried within walls. It is also common to find hot-water piping replaced by copper while the cold-water piping remains galvanized. Piping should be inspected in bathrooms, kitchens, and laundry areas, as well as in the basement.

The exposed cold-water piping is often wrapped with insulation to prevent condensation.

Copper piping should be supported with copper or plastic hangers. If another type of metallic hanger is used, localized rusting usually occurs where the dissimilar metals contact one another. Localized rusting also occurs at the connection of galvanized to copper pipe.

DRAINAGE SYSTEM

Drainage piping can be made of copper, ABS and PVC plastic, lead, galvanized steel, or cast iron. It is not uncommon to find several different types of drainage pipe used within a single house. Unlike the supply piping, where the water comes in under pressure, all water must exit from the drainage piping by gravity. Consequently, the pipes must have a reasonable slope.

PVC plastic piping has been commonly used in houses since the 1960s. This piping has a good track record; however, its life expectancy is not known. All indications are that it should last almost indefinitely. The single biggest drawback to plastic piping is that it tends to be noisy. Depending on the location of the main stack, loud water-rushing noises can be heard through the walls when a toilet is flushed.

Copper waste plumbing has all the virtues of copper supply piping. It is usually found in more expensive homes and in homes built immediately before plastic piping became common. Many older homes have a combination of drainage piping. The main waste stacks were generally made of cast iron. It is not uncommon to find cast-iron stacks in homes that are 80 to 100 years old with the pipe still in very good condition. Occasionally, pinhole leaks develop in this pipe; however, because the pipe is not under pressure, these holes are easily repaired with a rubber patch and a metal clamp.

Lead waste plumbing, commonly found in older homes, is usually restricted to the smaller lines running from fixtures to the main stack, although it was also used for larger waste lines running from toilets to the main stack. Because the water in contact with the pipe is running out of the house, there is no health hazard. However, lead waste piping can cause problems and inconvenience for it is difficult, if not impossible, to repair. Furthermore, because of its softness, it is easily deformed and therefore subject to mechanical damage. The first piece of lead waste piping commonly found during an inspection is below the laundry tubs in the basement.

Galvanized waste plumbing was commonly used in older homes on the vent piping for the waste plumbing system. Because these sections of pipe usually contain no water (only vapor), the rough, rusted inside of the pipe poses no serious problems. Waste venting pipes are larger in diameter than supply pipes and therefore rust-closure or rust-perforation problems are not typically encountered.

VENTING

For the waste plumbing system to function, it must be properly vented. If it isn't, water can be siphoned out of the traps below plumbing fixtures, allowing sewer gases to escape into the house.

The most obvious venting for the plumbing system is the continuation of the main waste stack up through the attic and the roof. Depending on the configuration of the plumbing system within the house, there may be more than one waste stack. Smaller vent pipes from various plumbing fixtures throughout the house usually tie into the main stack at some point above the level of the highest fixture within the house (see Figure 4.5). Because of the piping configuration and the wall finishes below the fixtures, much of the vent piping cannot be seen. Trying to determine its adequacy is very difficult. However, you should look for certain things. Generally, a stack vent should protrude through the roof approximately over the area of each toilet. Where a plumbing fixture is not close to a main stack, check the attic. A vent pipe above this fixture should run across the attic, joining the main stack. Some plumbing fixtures, because of their location, are difficult to vent. Sinks located in islands in the middle of kitchen areas should be studied carefully to determine if venting has been provided.

FIGURE 4.5 *Vent Terminology*

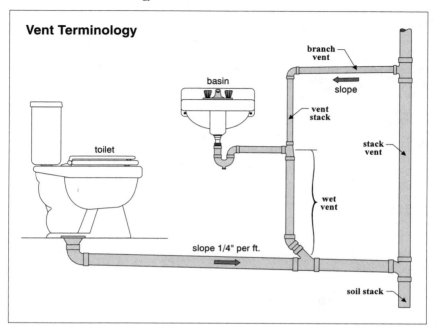

Vent Terminology

The location of the stacks protruding through the roof is important. Because the odors emitted from the stacks are unpleasant, it is best not to have stacks located near windows or roof decks.

The height and size of the stack are also important. In cold climates, the warm moist air rising up the stack tends to condense on the inside of the pipe where it protrudes above the roof. If the stack is high enough, frost could completely close the pipe, which would result in an unventilated plumbing system. Vent pipes are usually three or four inches in diameter where they protrude above the roof and should protrude no more than a foot.

FIXTURES

Every plumbing fixture within the house should be tested. The drains and undersides of all sinks should be inspected for leakage. The rate of drainage from fixtures should be checked. The caulking and tile work around bathtub enclosures should be thoroughly investigated.

FIGURE 4.6 *Pressure Decreases with Height*

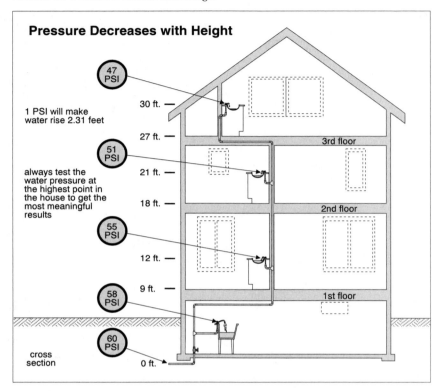

Water pressure within the house should also be tested (see Figure 4.6). Turn on the cold-water tap in the sink of the highest bathroom in the house. With the cold-water tap wide open, the cold water faucet at the bathtub should also be opened wide and the pressure drop at the sink should be noted. With the cold water faucets shut off, the same procedure should be followed for the hot-water taps. Two things should be noted: the actual drop in water pressure at the sink when the bathtub faucet is opened and the relative drop in water pressure at the sink between the hot- and cold-water pipes.

If the pressure drop is excessive, but nearly identical on the hot- and cold-water systems, the problem lies within the common plumbing upstream of the hot-water heater or evenly rusted galvanized plumbing throughout. If the pressure drop is more on one system than on the other, this indicates pressure problems within the piping of that particular section of the system. As further confirmation of your observations, it is best to flow the hot-water tap at the sink and the cold-water tap at the bathtub and vice versa to note the effect on the water pressure at the sink. If the water pressure at the sink is greatly affected, the restriction in the piping is in the common portion of the system.

This information can be correlated with what you have already observed about the location and amount of older galvanized pipe. A significant drop in water pressure indicates immediate replacement of the older pipe is necessary. This can be an expensive proposition. If, however, the pressure drop is not appreciable, and no leaks or rusty joints were noted during your visual inspection of the pipes, there are probably several years of life remaining in the pipes. Sometimes, water pressure problems are a result of undersized rather than corroded piping. Because all the water coming out of the faucets enters through one pipe, this pipe should ideally be larger than the pipes used downstream of the water heater when there is a hot- and cold-water pipe. In other words, the pipe upstream of the hot-water heater is carrying both the hot and the cold water, although the hot water has not yet become hot! Sometimes, this pressure drop can be rectified by simply increasing the diameter of this section of piping. Low water pressure can also be caused by an obstruction in the pipe, a partially closed valve, or a poor city water supply.

When inspecting the general interior finish of the house, try to correlate the location of water stains, if any, on interior walls and ceilings with the plumbing system. Sometimes what is thought to be a roof leak is damage resulting from a plumbing leak.

WASTE DISPOSAL SYSTEMS

In most municipalities, the waste plumbing is connected to sanitary sewers. The waste plumbing line simply exits below the basement floor and leads out to a larger pipe in the street. Obviously, a visual inspection of this section of the plumbing system is not possible.

The most common problem associated with this section of the plumbing system is a sewer backup. Several situations can cause a backup. For instance, there may be an inherent design problem in the entire sewage system in the area in which the house is located. In cases of this type, more waste enters the sewage system than can be carried away. Consequently, sewage water backs up through floor drains in the basements of houses. It can sometimes be difficult to determine whether this situation has occurred in the past and, more important, whether it is a recurring problem. Sometimes information can be gained from the seller, neighbors, or the municipality. Admittedly, information from these sources is often inconclusive.

Waste plumbing problems can also be more localized. They can be restricted to the main waste pipe for the house, as opposed to a regional problem. In this case, the problem is usually caused by a blocked or broken drainage pipe. Blockage can result from debris entering the waste system via floor drains and other plumbing fixtures, or it can be caused by roots from various trees and shrubbery. Drainage piping can also become broken by roots, frost heaving, or shifting of the pipe.

During the course of an inspection, there is no absolute means of testing the adequacy of the waste system. All that can be done is to flow an appreciable amount of water and note any backup. Evidence of problems may be found by looking at the clean-out cap on the main waste stack. If it has been recently opened, try to find out why.

Blocked drainage pipes can most often be corrected by a plumber with an eel or auger. A crushed drainage pipe requires digging down to the pipe to make the necessary repairs. While digging is obviously more expensive, a good plumber can usually locate the break and repair it without doing severe damage to the property or pocketbook.

SEPTIC SYSTEMS

In rural areas and in some suburban areas, waste disposal is handled by a septic system. A septic system consists of two major components: a tank (see Figure 4.7) and a disposal field. The tank is a watertight container usually made of concrete. It serves as a holding tank to allow solids that will not dissolve to settle to the bottom of the tank. Lighter materials that float are also held in the tank. The heavy solids are known as sludge and the lighter materials are known as scum. Within the tank, some of the solids are decomposed and are converted to a liquid. The liquid is discharged from the tank into the disposal field.

Disposal fields are also known as leaching beds (see Figure 4.8), tile beds, soil absorption fields, or drain fields. They consist of a network of perforated or open jointed pipes in trenches below the ground surface that allow the liquid waste (known as effluent) to percolate into the

FIGURE 4.7 *Septic Tank*

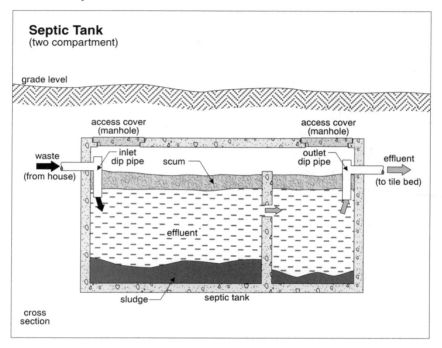

Septic Tank
(two compartment)

grade level

access cover (manhole)

access cover (manhole)

waste (from house)

inlet dip pipe

scum

outlet dip pipe

effluent (to tile bed)

effluent

sludge

septic tank

cross section

soil. The size of the leaching bed depends on the ability of the soil to absorb the effluent.

When inspecting a septic system, look for damp areas over the leaching bed and septic tank. Also note any objectionable smells. When the septic system fails, the porosity of the leaching bed is lost and can no longer absorb more effluent. Consequently, the effluent rises to the surface. When a leaching bed becomes plugged, a new leaching area must be built. One should ensure that there is sufficient room for a new area. With proper maintenance, a septic leaching area should last 20 to 30 years.

If possible, try to determine how frequently the septic tank has been cleaned of sludge. It should be inspected annually and cleaned every three to five years. If the tank is allowed to fill with sludge, solid waste will get into the leaching bed and plug it prematurely. This will probably result in effluent coming to the surface. If the system is completely plugged, and a significant amount of water is flowed within the house during the inspection, the lowest plumbing fixture in the house may back up.

FIGURE 4.8 *Tile Beds*

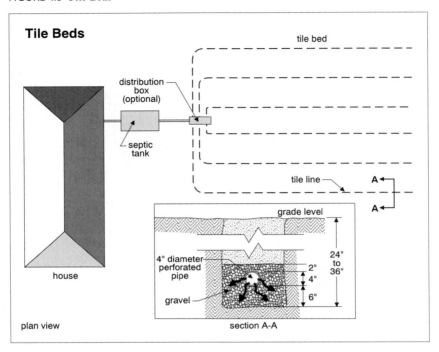

It is also important to determine the distance between a well and the septic tank and disposal system. Because the effluent that is discharged from the leaching field is far from pure, the well should be at least 50 feet from the septic tank and 100 feet from the disposal field.

SUMMARY

The most common major plumbing problem is worn-out galvanized supply piping. It is expensive to replace all the supply lines in a house. The cost is greater where the plumbing is covered by interior finishes.

Waste plumbing is not usually a source of major expense. Failed sections can be replaced on an as-needed basis. Similarly, venting deficiencies do not often result in expensive repairs. Replacing fixtures and remodeling kitchens and bathrooms can be the most expensive plumbing-related work. This is particularly true if fixtures are to be added or relocated.

A septic system is very costly to replace, particularly if there is no good location for a new tile bed.

CHECKLIST—The Plumbing

Water Supply: Private or public?

Private: Well location?
Pump type and condition?
Tank size and condition?
Short cycling of pump?

Public: Lead pipe from street to house?
Shutoff valve?

Distribution Piping

Copper or galvanized?
Size of main to hot-water heater?

Water heater: Electric?
Oil?
Gas?
Size?
Rental?
Copper or plastic hangers for copper pipe?

Drainage and Venting

Lead waste pipe?
Evidence of leakage?
Pipe condition?
Traps below fixtures?
Fixtures line up close to main vent?
Fixtures work properly?
Water pressure adequate?

Waste Disposal: Private or public?

Public: Evidence of sewer backup?
Clean-out on main stack recently opened?

Private: Age of septic system?
Damp areas over the tile bed or tank?
Odors?
Room for a new tile bed?
Separation between supply well and septic system?

5

THE HEATING SYSTEM

Many different types of heating systems are available residentially. Systems are classified by both the fuel they use and the medium they use to distribute the heat. Oil, natural gas, electricity, or solar energy can be used as fuel. Air, water, electric wiring, or sometimes steam can be used to distribute the heat. Different combinations of fuels and distribution systems are available; however, the warm-air furnace, the hot-water boiler, and electric heating are the most common.

WARM-AIR FURNACES

Warm-air furnaces are usually heated by oil or gas. While oil and gas furnaces may look somewhat different, they have several components in common. One such component is the heat exchanger. The flame itself and the by-products of combustion, such as water vapor, carbon monoxide, carbon dioxide, as well as sulfur, do not come in direct contact with the air used to heat the house (see Figure 5.1). Instead, the furnace has a heat exchanger. Heat exchangers come in many shapes and sizes, but, essentially, their purpose is to transfer the

FIGURE 5.1 *Heat Exchanger Heat Flow*

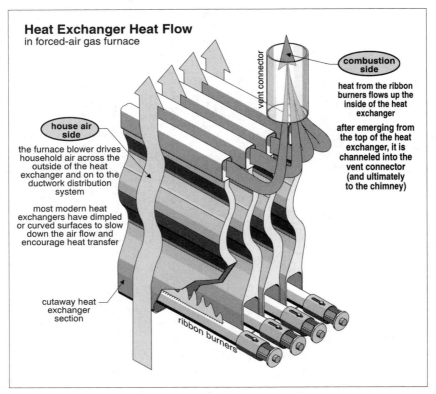

Heat Exchanger Heat Flow
in forced-air gas furnace

vent connector

combustion side

heat from the ribbon burners flows up the inside of the heat exchanger

after emerging from the top of the heat exchanger, it is channeled into the vent connector (and ultimately to the chimney)

house air side

the furnace blower drives household air across the outside of the heat exchanger and on to the ductwork distribution system

most modern heat exchangers have dimpled or curved surfaces to slow down the air flow and encourage heat transfer

cutaway heat exchanger section

ribbon burners

heat from the flame and hot gases to the air used to heat the house. The fuel is burned inside the heat exchanger, which is usually made of steel or cast iron. The distribution air is then allowed to pass across the outside of the heat exchanger to pick up the heat generated on the inside and distribute it throughout the house.

The heat exchanger is the most critical component of the furnace. If it should develop a leak by cracking or rusting through, then the products of combustion can leak through into the heat distribution system and come out of the air registers in the house. If enough leakage occurs, it results in odors and soot buildup, mostly visible around the registers. While heat exchangers can sometimes be replaced, it is more often necessary to replace the entire furnace.

Furnace Efficiencies

Conventional furnaces have an operating efficiency of about 80 percent. This means that about 20 percent of the heat is lost up the chimney. Considering the additional losses of maintaining the pilot light and warm air from the house going up the chimney when the furnace is off and during start-up and cooldown, the seasonal efficiency is typically 55 to 65 percent. These furnaces are no longer sold.

Midefficiency furnaces use vent dampers or induced draft fans and intermittent pilot lights to reduce the off-cycle losses. Efficiencies for these furnaces are typically 78 to 82 percent. In new installations, furnaces must be at least midefficiency.

High-efficiency furnaces have been around since the early 1980s. These furnaces condense the exhaust in an effort to get as much heat as possible out of the fuel. These units claim efficiencies of 85 to 95 percent. Although the cost to heat the house drops when a high-efficiency furnace is installed, this is often offset by the higher installation cost, as well as higher maintenance bills.

The life span of this new generation of efficient furnaces is not yet known, for they are still relatively new. These furnaces are more technically advanced than are their conventional efficiency predecessors. There are numerous fans, switches, relays, and circuit boards that did not exist on furnaces 25 years ago. Many of these midefficiency and high-efficiency furnaces have been redesigned several times in the past 15 years because of problems with less-than-perfect maintenance or installation.

The Distribution System

Besides the heat-generating section of the furnace, there is also a distribution system. Modern furnaces are forced-air systems (see Figure 5.2). This means a fan blows or forces the air across the heat exchanger, through the ductwork in the house, and into the various rooms through registers. The suction side of the fan is connected to return air ductwork, which draws air back out of the rooms to the furnace to be redistributed as warm air.

Older systems, called gravity furnaces, have no fan and rely on the principle that warm air will rise through the ductwork, forcing the colder, heavier air back to the furnace to be heated. These systems are

FIGURE 5.2 *House Air Flow*

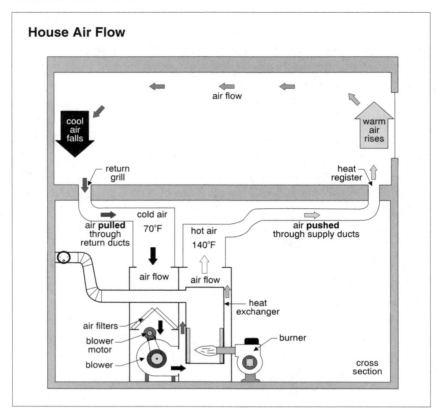

House Air Flow

far less efficient and rely on large, usually circular, ductwork to distribute the heat from a centrally located furnace known as an octopus (because of its huge ducts going off in all directions and looking much like a large mechanical octopus).

The distribution arrangement for either type of system, forced-air or gravity, should have ductwork that terminates in every room. Ideally, the supply air grilles should be located near exterior walls, preferably below windows, to provide the most heat to the coolest area of the room. On gravity systems, and early forced-air systems, this is often not the case for it involves the use of more ductwork.

Return air grilles to take the air back to the furnace should be plentiful (one per room located on the opposite side of the room from the supply air register), but seldom are, except in more expensive installations. They are quite often found centrally located on the first floor. In this case, it is important to have bedroom doors undercut by an inch or so to allow air to escape from the room and go back to the furnace. Otherwise, rooms with closed doors tend to get cold.

Inspection

If possible, test the furnace at the time of your inspection. Simply turn up the thermostat and see that the unit responds. On a forced-air system, the fan may take a few minutes to start (it waits for the furnace to get up to temperature). Listen for unusual noises and excessive vibration.

Look for rust, dirt, exposed poorly connected wiring, and general mechanical condition. A good percentage of furnace blowers have the date of manufacture stamped on the unit near an arrow showing the direction of rotation. While it is possible that the blower has been replaced, odds are good that this date represents the approximate date of manufacture of the furnace. Forced-air furnaces have an average life expectancy of 20 to 30 years. Octopus-style furnaces are, for the most part, obsolete. If you find one, plan on installing a new furnace and some new distribution ductwork in the near future.

Because forced-air furnaces physically move the air around the house, they are well suited to providing central humidification, electronic air cleaning, and air-conditioning.

Humidifying Systems

Central humidifiers are relatively inexpensive pieces of equipment that, when attached to a forced-air furnace, can add humidity to the air during dry winter months. There are many shapes and sizes, but two basic types are most common. The least expensive is the externally mounted drum-type (as shown in Figure 5.3). The unit is attached to the outside of the return-air ductwork with a bypass duct connected to the supply-air ductwork. It consists of a motor-operated drum, made of an absorbent material, which rotates in a tray of water where the water level is controlled by a float valve. The motor, which is controlled by a humidistat, rotates the drum only when the humidity levels are low. These humidifiers are often neglected and mineral deposits from the water clog up the tray and pads. Deposits also tend to clog the shutoff valve so that it does not completely turn off. The tray then overflows and water drips down onto the furnace ductwork. If the humidifier is mounted above

FIGURE 5.3 *Humidifier above Heat Exchanger*

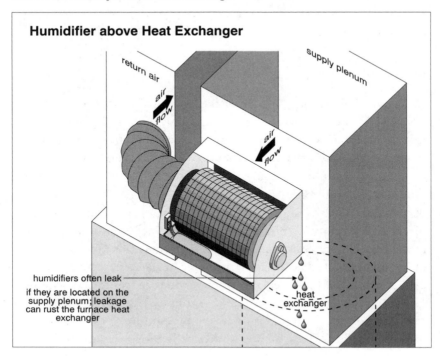

the furnace, the leakage can damage the heat exchanger or other components inside the furnace. This causes rusting and premature failure of the furnace.

A more desirable type of humidifier is the trickle type (see Figure 5.4). This consists of an electrically controlled water valve, which allows water to trickle down through a metal mesh pad. Air from the furnace is passed through this pad, where it picks up humidity. Excess water is collected and drained out of the unit through a small pipe. Because no water sits stagnant inside the humidifier, there is less opportunity for bacteria to grow. Regardless of which type of unit is used, it should be inspected carefully for leakage.

Electronic Air Cleaners

Electronic air filters clean the air to a much greater extent than conventional mechanical filters do. The unit is usually located on the return-air ductwork at a point where it meets the furnace. The unit has

FIGURE 5.4 *Trickle Humidifier*

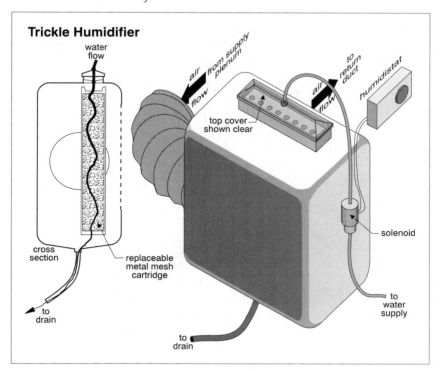

Trickle Humidifier

water flow

air from supply plenum

air flow

to return duct

humidistat

top cover shown clear

cross section

replaceable metal mesh cartridge

solenoid

to drain

to water supply

to drain

a preliminary mechanical filter to remove large pieces of debris. The smaller particles that get through the filter are electrically charged and then collected on plates of opposite polarity. Most units are equipped with test switches that should be checked. If functioning properly, a crackling noise will be heard. All units require regular maintenance and cleaning. Therefore, it is advisable to obtain the operating and maintenance book from the seller.

CENTRAL AIR-CONDITIONING

Central air-conditioning is a common feature on forced-air furnaces. Residential air-conditioning systems are usually composed of two separate sections (see Figure 5.5). One section—the evaporator coil—is located inside the ductwork immediately above the furnace. The refrigerant enters the coil in the ductwork in a liquid state and draws heat from the air to boil the liquid and turn it into a gas. This reduction in

FIGURE 5.5 *Air-Conditioning–Schematic of System*

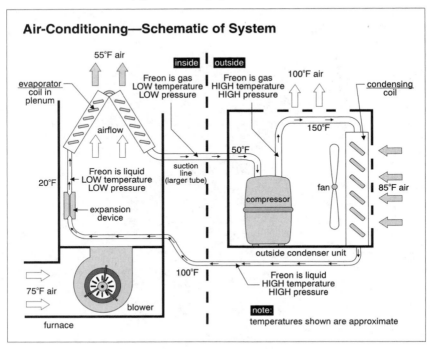

air temperature also causes condensation on the coil, reducing humidity levels. The condensate is collected in a tray and allowed to drain out of the unit. The condensate drain line usually runs down the outside of the furnace to a nearby floor drain.

The other half of the unit is located outdoors, if it is an air-cooled system. This section consists of a compressor and a condenser coil, which converts the refrigerant gas back into a liquid state by compressing it and allowing it to give off heat to the outdoors. A compressor has an average life of 10 to 15 years. It is the heart of the system.

Some systems are water-cooled rather than air-cooled. In this case, the unit containing the condenser and compressor is usually located indoors near the furnace. Rather than giving off heat to the outdoors, the heat is removed by water. The units tend to last longer for they are not subjected to the elements and extreme temperatures. However, the water used for cooling is usually domestic water that goes down the drain. The water has to be paid for—which increases the expense of operation—and cannot be reused except for such things as watering lawns.

Systems with outside compressors should not be tested when temperatures are below 60°F (15°C) for this can cause severe damage to the unit. It is best to get permission from the owner to test either type of unit because difficulties can arise with units that have been shut down for several months.

When testing air-conditioning systems, simply set thermostat controls for cooling. Check for cool air from the registers and warm air from the outside condenser unit. On water systems, listen for water running through the unit and down the drain. Also, check for unusual noises from the compressor and the fan unit. Even under normal circumstances, some units are quite noisy, so it is a good idea to listen to the neighbor's unit as well as your own.

In houses with hot-water heat, sometimes an independent air-conditioning system is installed in the attic and ductwork is run through the attic space and down the walls. This ductwork must be insulated. Attic units should also be contained in a drip pan to prevent water damage to the ceilings if the condensate line should get plugged. These units should be tested for excessive noise and vibration.

There are also some independent air-conditioners that have no ducts. These units are mounted on the interior walls of the home and look like high-quality window-mounted air-conditioners. These ductless systems are connected to outside coils that are similar to those used for conventional systems. There may be one or several of these units in a home, placed in strategic areas.

HEAT PUMPS

Heat pumps are quite popular in some areas of North America, depending on the climate. A heat pump is a central air-conditioning system that cools the house in the summer and can be used to add heat to the house during the heating season. This is essentially accomplished by reversing the refrigerant flow through the air-conditioning system. During relatively mild weather, a heat pump can be a very efficient system for adding heat to a house. As the weather becomes colder, however, a heat pump alone cannot supply sufficient heat for a home. A furnace or electric baseboard heaters are still needed in addition to a heat pump.

Under normal circumstances, the heat pump is set to shut off at a certain temperature (usually around the freezing point) and the fur-

FIGURE 5.6 *Typical Compressor Life*

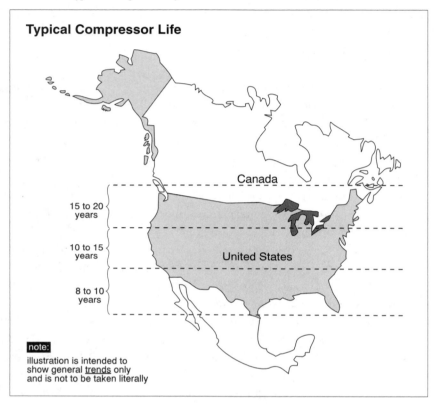

nace takes over. Electric furnaces allow simultaneous operation of both the furnace and heat pump, while gas or oil furnaces must run alone.

Generally speaking, a heat pump may be considered cost-effective in mild climates if an air-conditioning system is to be provided in any case. While heat pumps are more expensive than air-conditioning systems, the added cost may be recouped in a reasonable time, depending on several factors.

The life expectancy of a heat pump compressor is similar to that of an air-conditioning compressor. Many heat pump compressors are installed inside the home, which protects them from extremes in weather. On the other hand, heat pumps are expected to operate more than air-conditioners, for they provide heat as well. A 10- to 20-year life span is projected (see Figure 5.6).

The inspection procedures for a heat pump are similar to those for an air-conditioning system. A heat pump should not be operated in the

FIGURE 5.7 *How Boilers Work*

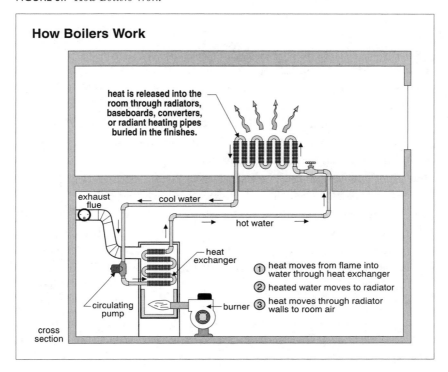

How Boilers Work

heat is released into the room through radiators, baseboards, converters, or radiant heating pipes buried in the finishes.

exhaust flue

cool water

hot water

heat exchanger

① heat moves from flame into water through heat exchanger

② heated water moves to radiator

③ heat moves through radiator walls to room air

circulating pump

burner

cross section

cooling mode at temperatures below 65°F (18°C) nor should it be operated in the heating mode at temperatures above 60°F (15°C).

HOT-WATER HEATING SYSTEMS

Hot-water heating systems (also known as hydronic heating) are common in older houses. As with warm-air systems, the most common fuels are gas and oil. Many older hot-water furnaces (boilers) were once coal-fired or wood-fired, but have since been converted to a more convenient fuel. As with warm-air systems, the boiler has a heat exchanger to transfer the heat generated within the furnace to the water (see Figure 5.7). Again, the heat exchanger is the most critical component of the boiler. If it develops a crack or a hole, water will leak into the combustion chamber. Depending on the type of boiler, there may be a large access door into the combustion area or there may be only a small observation port. If possible, look inside the combustion area for water accumulation or rust stains from a leak. When looking inside, also check the condition of the refractory material in the firebox. The refractory material is a type of brick designed for high temperatures. It deteriorates with time and eventually needs rebuilding. If you cannot look inside, listen for hissing noises from boiling droplets of water immediately after the boiler has shut off. If there is a leak in the heat exchanger, the heating plant will most likely have to be replaced.

If at all possible, try to establish the age of the unit. Older cast-iron boilers were originally designed for coal. These large heavy boilers may be circular or rectangular and are usually assembled in sections. Sometimes the entire boiler is wrapped with insulation to keep the heat inside. They have an average life of 35 to 50 years. Unlike other types of heating systems that seem to fail like clockwork within a given time span, however, many cast-iron boilers remain in service for 70 or 80 years. Their efficiency, however, tends to decrease with age. Scale and rust that build up on the heat exchanger inhibit the flow of heat from the flame to the water. Therefore, even though the unit has not failed, if it is over 50 or 60 years old, it might be wise to replace it simply to gain the efficiency of a new unit. Older cast-iron boilers have an average efficiency rating in the neighborhood of 60 percent. More conventional late-model hot-water boilers have efficiencies in the 80 percent range. Some new types of boilers coming onto the market claim a 95 percent efficiency rating.

During the 1940s and 1950s, hot-water boilers were undergoing changes. Steel boilers became popular and both steel and cast-iron boilers became more compact and were enclosed in sheet metal covers. The life expectancy of a steel boiler is somewhat less than that of cast iron—20 to 35 years for old units and 15 to 25 years for the newer, lighter units. If it is not possible to determine whether the heat exchanger is cast iron or steel, note the name and model number and check with the manufacturer.

A third type of hot-water boiler became popular through the 1960s and 1970s. This boiler, which is enclosed in a very compact metal cabinet, has a copper heat exchanger. Because of a rapid transfer of heat from the flame to the water, only a small heat exchanger is needed. The life expectancy of these is 15 to 25 years.

Also associated with boilers are various limit switches and safety devices. These devices sense water temperature, flue gas temperature, water levels, etc., to ensure the safe operation of the boiler. It is beyond the scope of this book to deal adequately with the various types of safety equipment on heating systems.

FIGURE 5.8 *Closed Hydronic System*

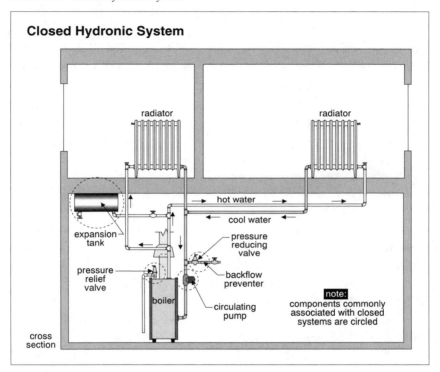

The Distribution System

Many older heating systems rely on gravity to distribute the water. Warm water, which is relatively light, simply rises through the pipes to the radiators forcing the colder, heavier water back to the boiler (see Figure 5.8). On all new hot-water systems, circulating pumps are provided. These pumps can also be added to older boilers on a retrofit basis. Rather than relying on the water to travel by gravity, the pumps circulate the water through the heating system. Whether the water is distributed by gravity or with a pump, an expansion tank is included in the system. This tank, which is partially filled with air, allows the water to expand as it is heated.

The distribution piping for the hot-water system should be looked at closely. Quite often distribution pipes are insulated in the basement area to prevent excessive heat loss from the pipes before they get to the radiators. Most distribution piping problems occur at the connection to the radiators and not in the piping itself. However, the pipes are very costly to replace and should be inspected carefully for rust and leakage.

The heating pipes terminate at radiators or convectors. Radiators are usually made of cast iron and are very heavy, and they give off relatively even heat because of their mass. A control valve on the piping at the radiator allows the heat to be regulated by adjusting the amount of hot water flowing through the radiator. A smaller air bleed valve at the top of the radiator allows the release of any air trapped in the system. Air in a radiator will prevent hot water from entering the unit. Occasionally, the radiators themselves leak, but most problems are associated with sticky or leaking control valves and bleed valves. On an individual basis, they are not costly to repair, but it can become expensive if most valves need work.

Convectors are usually found in newer homes and tend to give off heat more efficiently through thin metal fins. The heating is more cyclical for the units do not retain much heat when the boiler is not on. Besides checking the valves, look for damaged fins, which will reduce efficiency.

As with forced-air heat, make sure there is a sufficient number of radiators or convectors throughout the house. Ideally, there should be at least one per room. It should be located by an exterior wall below a window, if possible. If one or two cool areas are noted, electric baseboard heaters can usually be added inexpensively.

FORCED-AIR HEATING VERSUS HOT-WATER HEATING

Forced-air heating is not inherently better than hot-water heating and vice versa. Both furnaces and boilers have advantages relative to each other.

Advantages of Forced-Air Heating

1. A forced-air heating system is more versatile than a hot-water system. The same distribution system can be used to cool, clean, humidify, and dehumidify the air. With hot-water heating systems, this is not possible.

2. Forced-air heating systems generally have lower installation costs than do hot-water heating systems.
3. Forced-air systems generally have lower maintenance costs.
4. Warm-air heating systems tend to respond faster. If the house is cool, a warm-air system will bring it up to temperature very quickly. Hot-water systems are slower to respond.
5. Within each room, forced-air systems take up less space. A heating register located on the floor or the wall does not interfere with the furniture layout as much as a radiator or convector does.
6. If the heating system should fail, there is no danger of freezing heating pipes as there is with a hot-water system.
7. During renovation work, it is much easier to relocate a warm-air register and its associated ductwork than to relocate a radiator.

Advantages of Hot-Water Heating

1. While warm-air systems tend to respond faster, they are also more cyclical. The temperature within the house tends to rise and fall as the furnace goes on and off. The heat retention of a large cast-iron radiator dampens this cycling effect so that the heat from a hot-water system is much more even.
2. While forced-air systems take less space within a given room, they require more space (in basements and within walls and floors) for ductwork than hot-water heating systems take for piping.
3. Hot-water heating systems tend to be quieter than forced-air systems, which make more noise as the ductwork expands and contracts. Fans on forced-air heating systems can also be noisy.
4. On some forced-air systems, the movement of the air from the registers creates drafts within the house. No real air movement is experienced with a hot-water system, with the exception of slow convection of the heat given off by the radiators.
5. It may be easier to extend a hot-water system because pipes are easier to add and the capacity of the system is generally larger and can accept a heavier load.
6. While hot-water systems do have higher installation costs, they have longer life expectancies as well.

FIGURE 5.9 *Equivalent Furnaces*

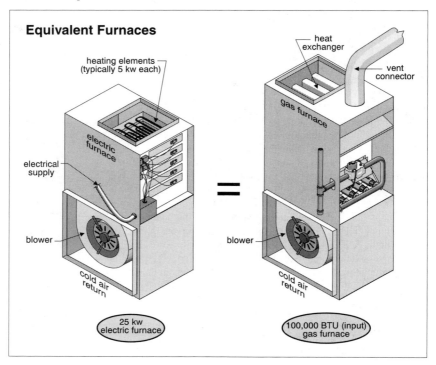

7. When a forced-air system fails, products of combustion from the unit may get into the main air stream of the house. This problem is eliminated with the use of hot-water piping.

ELECTRIC HEATING

There are many ways to use electricity to heat a house. One way is to use a forced-air furnace, as described earlier. Instead of a flame and a heat exchanger, electric resistance wires are used. Because there are no products of combustion, the wires can sit right in the air stream above the blower, eliminating the need for a heat exchanger. Electric forced-air furnaces have longer life expectancies than fuel-fired furnaces; however, components such as heating wires, fans, and blowers may have to be replaced for they wear out. Electric furnaces have another advantage over coal oil, or gas furnaces because they do not require chimneys (see Figure 5.9).

FIGURE 5.10 *Best Location for Electric Heaters*

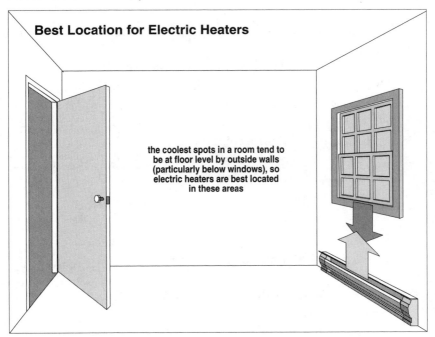

Best Location for Electric Heaters

the coolest spots in a room tend to
be at floor level by outside walls
(particularly below windows), so
electric heaters are best located
in these areas

The most common form of electric heat is baseboard resistance heaters. Electric baseboard heaters should be located on exterior walls, preferably below windows (see Figure 5.10). Units are usually individually controlled by a dial right on the heater or by wall-mounted thermostats. The wall-mounted thermostat is preferred because it is more convenient. It can be a real nuisance to reach the control mounted right on a baseboard unit.

Each unit should be checked for proper operation. If one or two do not work, it isn't a serious problem for they are not particularly expensive items. In that sense, baseboard heat is advantageous because all your eggs are not in one basket (as with an expensive furnace) but rather spread throughout the house.

Because the number of units necessary to provide heat varies because of climate and building insulation, no rule of thumb can be given; however, you should note rooms that do not have any heaters or that need more units.

Advantages of Electric Baseboard Heat

1. There is no distribution network as such, simply wires requiring little space.
2. There is no single major component to fail.
3. Individual thermostats provide good control of temperature, room by room.
4. There is no risk from products of combustion within the house.
5. There is no need for a chimney.
6. The system is not susceptible to damage by freezing.
7. Electric baseboard heat is quick to respond.
8. Electric heating is very quiet.
9. It has a low installation cost.

Disadvantages of Electric Baseboard Heat

1. There is no ability to cool, humidify, and clean the air, for there is no ductwork system.
2. Historically, electric heating has been more expensive than other systems to operate.
3. A larger electrical system is required.

Some houses are heated electrically with radiant ceiling panels. These panels consist of resistance wiring embedded in the ceiling during installation or installed in prewired panels (see Figure 5.11). Radiant heating has advantages because there are no obvious heating sources in the room to interfere with furniture layout. However, it does have some drawbacks. Because radiant ceiling heating can be considered much like the radiant heating you receive when sitting out in the sunlight, areas in the shade tend to be rather cool. This phenomenon can occur when sitting at a large table, for example. The area under the table will be "in the shade" and so it will be significantly cooler.

The second and perhaps greater disadvantage with radiant ceiling panels is that they are difficult to repair. If one of the wires proves faulty and there is a break in the circuit, it is hard to isolate the problem to make the necessary repairs. In that sense, it is also very difficult to inspect a system of this type when you are performing a prepurchase analysis. All you can do is turn on the units and attempt to feel the heat.

FIGURE 5.11 *Electric Radiant Heat–Ceilings*

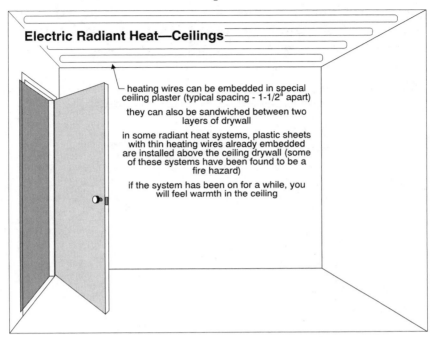

Electric Radiant Heat—Ceilings

heating wires can be embedded in special ceiling plaster (typical spacing - 1-1/2" apart)

they can also be sandwiched between two layers of drywall

in some radiant heat systems, plastic sheets with thin heating wires already embedded are installed above the ceiling drywall (some of these systems have been found to be a fire hazard)

if the system has been on for a while, you will feel warmth in the ceiling

The surface temperature of the ceiling will be somewhat higher than the temperature in the room.

Radiant ceiling panels can also be installed using hot-water pipes as opposed to electric wires. The same principle applies, except that a leak in the system is much easier to detect than a broken electric wire. Unfortunately, there is also more potential for damage to furniture and room finishes.

Radiant heat, either electric or hot water, can also be installed in the floor. Once again, locating defects can be difficult, especially if the system is embedded in a concrete floor.

SUMMARY

This chapter has touched on the most common types of heating systems, although there are many more variations, from gas-fired wall furnaces to hot-water radiant floor heating to steam boilers. You may want to talk with local specialists if you come across a type of heating system that you are not familiar with.

Obviously, the heating system is an important component of the house. The heating plant itself, whether a warm-air furnace or hot-water boiler, is expensive to replace. Problems with the distribution network are less likely; however, the adequacy of the distribution network should be analyzed. While there are pros and cons to the various types of heating systems, none is a clear-cut winner. Therefore, the type of system within the house should not be a major concern.

CHECKLIST—The Heating System

Warm-Air Furnaces

1. Gravity or forced?

2. Age?

3. Fuel?

4. Condition?

5. Adequate distribution?

6. Humidifier leakage?

7. Central air-conditioning: Type?
   Age?
   Condition?
   Noise?

8. Heat pumps: Age?
   Condition?
   Noise?

9. Electronic air filter?

Hot-Water Boiler

1. Circulating pump?

2. Age?

3. Fuel?

4. Condition?

5. Adequate distribution?

6. Radiator condition: Valves?
   Leakage?

7. Convector condition: Fins?
   Valves?
   Leakage?

Electric Baseboard Heat

1. Condition of each unit?

2. Adequate number of units?

6

THE BASEMENT AND CRAWL SPACE

Dampness or water in basements and crawl spaces is the source of great frustration for homeowners. Because it is not an unusual problem and can be complicated to address, you'll want to inspect carefully for this issue and understand its causes, implications, and solutions when making a purchase decision.

WET BASEMENTS

Water can find its way into the basement from two primary sources (see Figure 6.1). The first is surface water, which includes rain runoff and melted snow. The second is subsurface water (groundwater) from a high-water table or an underground spring or stream.

The first is by far the most common source of wet basements and the one most readily prevented. Subsurface water problems are often difficult to resolve, but, fortunately, they are fairly rare.

Evidence of Water Problems

Most basements with moisture problems are not wet all the time. Consequently, you will have to look for clues in the basement (see Fig-

FIGURE 6.1 *Causes of Wet Basement Problems*

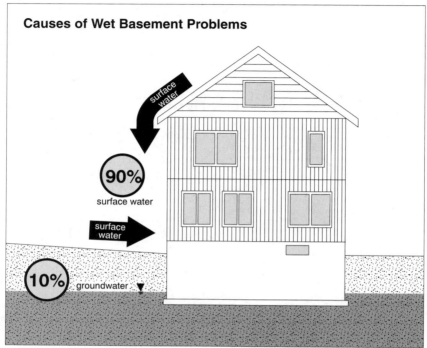

ure 6.2). One of the best clues is whether valuables are stored directly on the basement floor. If wooden furniture and cardboard boxes, for instance, have been sitting on the floor for some time and show no evidence of damage, this is a good indication that the basement is relatively dry. If, on the other hand, everything is raised on wood planks or platforms, one may be justifiably suspicious.

Unfinished basement walls also provide clues. Look for water stains or paint that has peeled, particularly on the lower section of the walls. Sometimes a white powdery crystal is found on the walls. This efflorescence is a salt deposit left by the water that evaporates from the wall surface. The salts have been dissolved by the water as it passes through the foundation wall. This is an indication of water seepage, but may not represent a severe leakage problem. Be on the lookout for other clues. If the basement has recently been painted, concentrate on out-of-the-way areas.

Check for water stains or rust under the stairs, below furnaces and water heaters, behind laundry tubs, in cupboards and cold-storage

FIGURE 6.2 *Wet Basement Clues–Part 1*

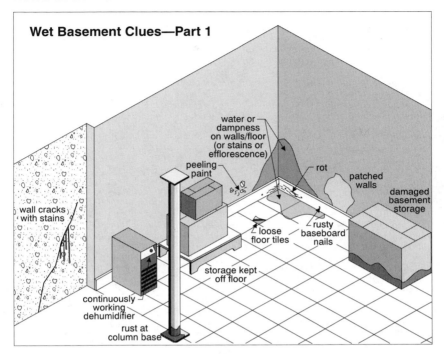

Wet Basement Clues—Part 1

water or dampness on walls/floor (or stains or efflorescence)

peeling paint

rot

patched walls

damaged basement storage

wall cracks with stains

loose floor tiles

rusty baseboard nails

storage kept off floor

continuously working dehumidifier

rust at column base

rooms. A word of caution about rust around furnaces: Be careful not to confuse the rust caused by a leaking humidifier with the rust from water on the floor. Water from a humidifier will produce vertical streaking or rusting down one side of the furnace. Water on the floor will attack only the bottom of the furnace, but on all sides.

Where wood is found near floor level, such as at the bottom of stairs or posts, look for water stains and rot. A probe may be useful in this investigation. The joint between the floor and the wall is another common leakage point that should be checked.

Where the basement is finished, look at the bottom of paneling for dark streaks, rot, mold and mildew, or deformation of the wallboard. Rust around nail heads and electrical outlets are other signs. Staining and rusting may also appear behind and below electric baseboard heaters.

White efflorescence may be noted between floor tiles, indicating water below the floor. If a wood subfloor has been laid, walk the entire floor and watch for soft or springy areas. These, too, may mean water trouble below. If the floor is carpeted, a musty odor may be a clue that water problems have been experienced.

FIGURE 6.3 *Wet Basement Clues–Part 2*

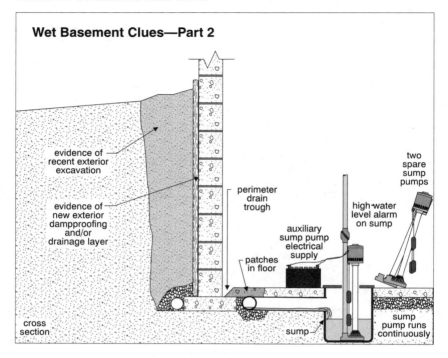

Wet Basement Clues—Part 2

If the foundation walls are poured concrete, look for vertical rusty streaks. They generally indicate water leakage through the holes left by the form tie-rods that were inserted when the wall was put up. (When a concrete wall is erected, rods are used to hold forms in place. When the rods are removed, holes are left in the wall.) These holes should be patched with concrete or hydraulic cement, preferably from the outside as well as the inside.

Most cracking in basement floors is not a major problem. It is sometimes because of water below the floor, but usually does not affect the structural integrity of the house. If the water below is removed, the process is usually arrested. Sometimes, however, soil can settle or be eroded from below the concrete, creating an unsafe condition. Tap the floor and listen for a hollow sound. With a little practice, you will be able to identify an underfloor soil problem. (See Figure 6.3 for more clues about wet basements.)

FIGURE 6.4 *Control Surface Water*

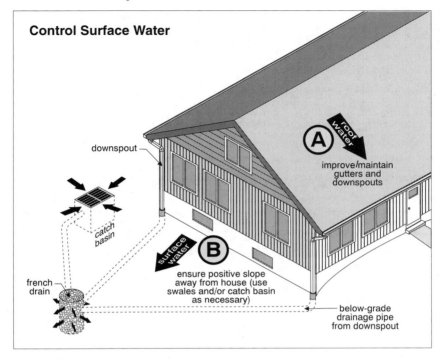

Causes and Solutions

In many cities, some evidence of moisture penetration can be found in almost every house. As discussed, the culprit is usually surface water. While there are a multitude of remedies available, the best solution is to eliminate the problem at the source. If you can keep water from collecting around the basement walls, you should be able to prevent leakage. You can accomplish this by ensuring that the land adjacent to the building slopes down away from the house. As discussed in Chapter 1, the land should slope down approximately one inch per foot for the first six feet away from the building (see Figure 6.4). All surfaces, including lawns, gardens, driveways, patios, and sidewalks, should be included in this slope. If the property hasn't been landscaped in this way, correcting the slope of the land can be a relatively expensive proposition. This is particularly true where patios, sidewalks, and driveways have to be reworked.

If there appear to be water problems, you should also check the gutters and downspouts. Again, we talked about this system in Chapter 1. Collecting the water from the roof system and discharging it into a localized area outside the foundation wall almost always leads to moisture problems in the basement. The first thing is to ensure that all the roof water is being collected. Gutters may have to be cleaned, realigned, repaired, replaced, or added. Second, downspouts must either carry the water into a house waste system or discharge it several feet away from the house.

In many city homes, built from the 1940s onward, drainage tile has been laid around the base of the foundation walls outside the house. This tile may be a red-orange clay tile or a perforated plastic pipe. The drainage system is designed to prevent water from standing in the soil outside the foundation wall. Water enters the pipe at joints between the sections of clay tile or through the holes in the plastic pipe. The tile is covered with gravel to allow water to reach the tile easily and enter the drainage system. The water collected is discharged into a sewer system or a sump from which it may be pumped away from the building.

These drainage systems are valuable, but they do not compensate for poor grading or inadequate gutters and downspouts. In many houses 25 years old or more, the tile is broken or clogged with soil and/or tree roots. Water from a partially fouled tile system outside three of the foundation walls can all end up at the fourth wall where the tile is clogged. This can aggravate rather than relieve moisture problems in the basement. In some cases, it is necessary to dig down to the base of the foundation walls to repair an existing drainage system, or to add one if none is found. This is only necessary, however, where the above-grade solutions we have previously discussed are not effective.

Basement windows can allow water to enter, too. Poorly arranged windows at or below grade will allow rainwater and melted snow to seep in. Look closely at window frames and at wall areas immediately below. Evidence of water will show up as staining, efflorescence, or paint peeling on the walls and as discoloration or rot on the window frames. Incidentally, this area is highly susceptible to termite infestation, so remember to look for the shelter tubes or wood damage.

Where the bottom of the basement window is at or below grade, a window well may be necessary (see Figure 6.5). The well should be large enough to permit light passing through the window and allow easy

FIGURE 6.5 *Drain Problems*

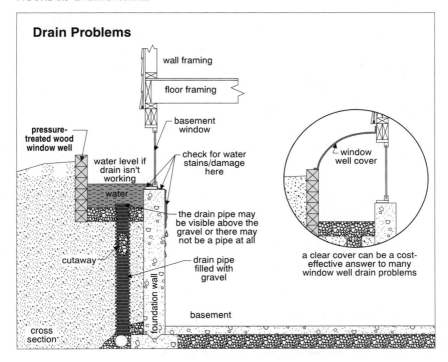

access for cleaning both the well and the window. A concrete or corrugated steel shell is commonly used to form the well, although chemically treated lumber is sometimes employed successfully.

To drain the well, usually a vertical pipe filled with gravel discharges into the foundation drainage tile or to a dry well (a large volume of gravel below grade that allows water to collect and percolate slowly into the soil). Where a solid drainage pipe has been provided, the ground level in the window well should not be lower than the top of the drainage pipe, otherwise water will not flow into the pipe. Where coarse soils are found, no additional drainage may be necessary. However, the base of the well should slope away from the house.

Although window wells should be kept free of debris, they are often neglected. In some cases, the well drainage system is blocked and moisture problems appear despite the presence of the well. The easiest solution may be to install a clear plastic dome cover over the well to prevent water accumulation. This allows light to pass through, but does prevent basement ventilation.

Another cause of dampness in basements is a poorly arranged outside stairwell. A drain should be provided in a landing at the base of the stairwell. A six-inch door threshold will help prevent water and snow from getting in around the door. Anything less can result in problems. Look at the bottom of the basement door for signs of water damage. Open the basement door and take a good look at the stairwell. Cracking and heaving caused by frost action are common problems. Rebuilding a damaged basement stairwell is a difficult and expensive chore. There should be a hand railing on the stairs, but often there isn't.

Sometimes one very distinct waterline can be seen in the basement. Where this well-defined stain is noted and there is no other evidence of water damage, it is possible that a one-time flood has occurred. This may be the result of a laundry tub overflowing, a leak in the water pipes, a sewer backup, a ruptured water heater or boiler, or some other incident. Sometimes this can be explained by the previous owner and should not necessarily be cause for alarm.

Other Basement Features

A basement should have a floor drain and the floor should slope toward it. Where possible, check that there is water in the trap by looking straight down the drain. If no water is seen, the trap may be cracked or broken. It is also possible that the water in the trap has just evaporated. Pour a bucket of water down the drain; if no water stays in the trap, minor repairs will be necessary.

On newer houses, a trap primer (see Figure 6.6) is often provided. This is a small hose, usually plastic, that is connected to a faucet that is used regularly. The other end of the hose discharges into the drain above the trap. For example, where laundry tubs are provided in the basement, a hose is often connected to the cold-water tap. When the tap is open, water flows into the floor drain, replenishing any water that has evaporated from the trap.

If a laundry area is located in the basement, flow some water into the tubs. Many of the older concrete tubs with lead waste piping leak in at least one place. Faucets may be inoperative, or the supply piping may be badly deteriorated. A second set of faucets with threaded ends can be used to connect a washing machine. An ordinary 120-volt electrical outlet is adequate to power the washer. Look for a heavy-duty electric

FIGURE 6.6 *Trap Primer*

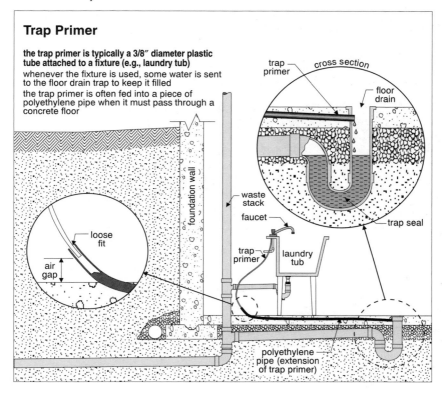

Trap Primer

the trap primer is typically a 3/8″ diameter plastic tube attached to a fixture (e.g., laundry tub)

whenever the fixture is used, some water is sent to the floor drain trap to keep it filled

the trap primer is often fed into a piece of polyethylene pipe when it must pass through a concrete floor

trap primer   cross section

floor drain

waste stack

faucet

trap primer   laundry tub

trap seal

loose fit

air gap

foundation wall

polyethylene pipe (extension of trap primer)

supply or a gas hookup for a clothes dryer. If a clothes dryer is in place, it should be vented to the exterior.

A sump pump may also be found in the basement. This pump is located in a sump or pit below the basement floor level and is designed to remove water from around basement walls and below the basement floor (see Figure 6.7). Sometimes gutter and downspout water is also handled by a sump pump. Most often provided where the water table is high during the spring or where there are no storm sewers, sump pumps can also be used to get rid of water inside the house. A floor drain may carry water into the sump from a malfunctioning washing machine, leaking pipes, etc. The pump may discharge into a ditch at the front of the property, onto the lawn surface, or into a dry well below grade. In any case, the water should be carried well away from the building before it is released.

The pump is usually controlled by a float valve and can be operated by lifting the float. However, this should only be done if there is water

FIGURE 6.7 *Why Is There a Sump Pump in the Basement?*

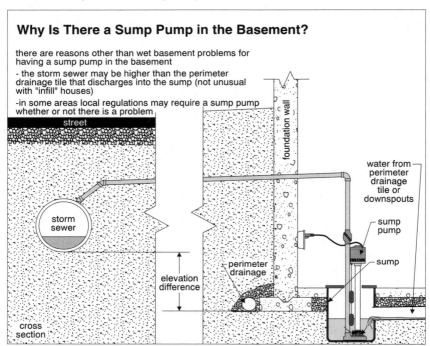

in the sump that can be pumped! The pump should start and the water level should drop. Make sure the pump shuts down automatically. Check the electrical connections to a sump pump, which are often poor.

An auxiliary pump that is powered by the pressure of the water in the supply plumbing is sometimes added. This type of pump is used in the case of an electrical failure or a malfunction of the electric pump. You can readily identify it by the connection to the water supply plumbing in the house and a lack of electrical wiring. It can be tested by opening the water supply valve to the pump. This type of pump, sometimes referred to as an ejector pump, is also activated by a float valve.

Finished Basements

Sometimes an unfinished basement can be improved to add living space and value to a home. In some cases, a basement apartment can be created. If you have plans for the basement, consider these basic requirements. The ceiling height should be at least seven feet over most of the area to be finished. Windows should be provided, both for light

FIGURE 6.8 *Lowering Basement Floors–Bench Footing*

Lowering Basement Floors—Bench Footing

wall framing

floor framing

topsoil

foundation wall

backfill

original footing

original floor level

original drainage tile

new concrete floor slab

new concrete bench footing

45°

gravel

cross section

new interior drainage tile sometimes installed

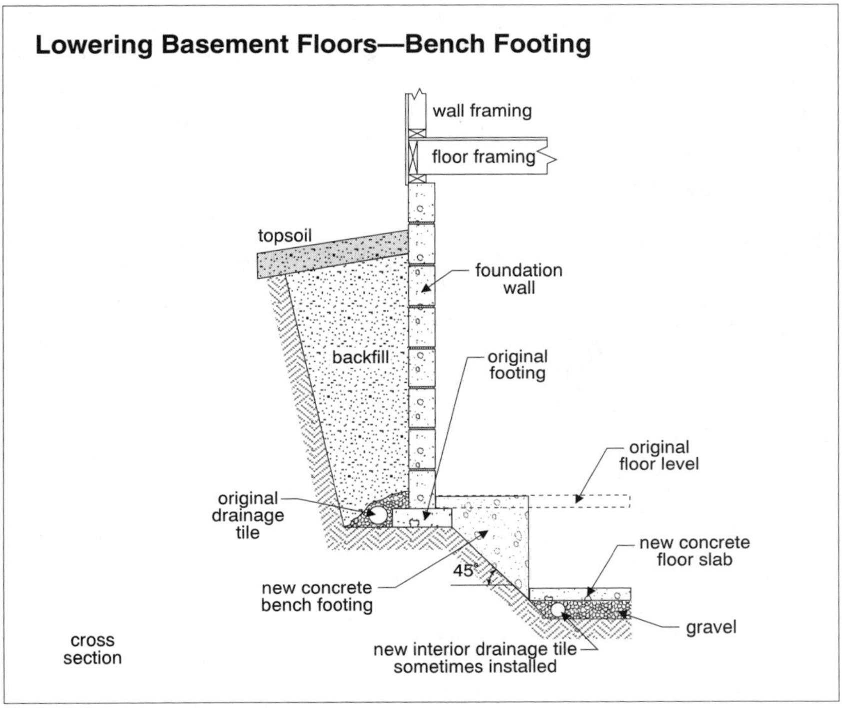

and ventilation. The furnace and mechanical room will have to be partitioned off. It may be necessary to extend the heating system, if it has adequate capacity. Alternatively, electric resistance baseboard heaters can be added. These are relatively inexpensive to install, but electric heat may be expensive to operate.

If an apartment is planned, check municipal requirements thoroughly. Requirements for height, windows, fire separations, fire exits, and local zoning are only some of the areas that should be investigated. In many jurisdictions, air cannot be transferred from one living unit to another through heating ductwork. This prevents simply extending a forced-air heating system to warm a basement. In some locales, the basement must have some area at grade level to be usable as a living area. The size of the electrical service should also be considered. A heavier service and/or separate meters may be necessary.

Where basement height is inadequate, it may be possible to lower the basement floor (see Figure 6.8). This, however, should be done with the assistance of a professional. Depending on the additional depth needed, problems may be encountered with footings or with the waste plumbing system. Below most foundation walls and support posts are the footings, or pads, which help spread the load and keep the building from sinking. If the floor is lowered indiscriminately, these footings can be broken off or undermined. This may seriously compromise the support for the building. Often the floor is lowered in the central areas only, leaving a ledge around the walls. This configuration is sometimes referred to as a Dutch wall or a bench footing. In some homes, the waste plumbing pipes run just under the basement floor with a very gentle slope toward the street sewer. Lowering the basement floor level can necessitate running this pipe inside the room area. Again, professional advice should be sought before beginning work.

If you are inspecting a house with a basement apartment, it is wise to have your lawyer verify its acceptability.

CRAWL SPACES

Some houses do not have full basements. There may be a partial basement plus a crawl space or only a crawl space. This area is accessible from the basement, from a trapdoor in the floor above, or from outside the building. The crawl space is perhaps the most difficult area to inspect in a house, because of lack of space; it is also among the most important. As discussed in Chapter 2, it is necessary to check the foundations and framing members for evidence of structural problems. Heating ductwork and plumbing pipes that run through the crawl space may be rusted or disconnected. Electrical wiring should also be followed and examined visually, where possible.

The depth of the crawl space should be at least two feet, and preferably more, to facilitate access. The crawl space floor is often earth, although it may be gravel, wood, or concrete. Sometimes shallow crawl spaces are provided with trenches, allowing access to the mechanical systems. This is a less desirable arrangement. Where the crawl space floor is earth, look for a vapor barrier of plastic sheeting or roll roofing covering the floor surface (see Figure 6.9). This will prevent moisture from migrating upwards from the soil into the crawl space. Where there is no vapor barrier, look very closely for signs of rot in wood components of the crawl space.

FIGURE 6.9 *Cover Crawl Space Floor*

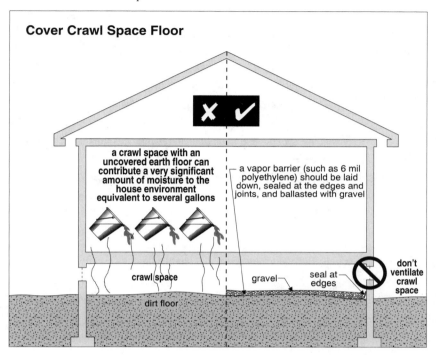

Two philosophies commonly are employed for crawl space insulation. The first is to consider the crawl space as the outdoors. Here the underside of the floors above should be insulated (to approximately R-26) as discussed in Chapter 8. The insulation should be fitted into the joist spaces of the floor and should be well secured in place. Using chicken wire mesh is very satisfactory. The vapor barrier should be on the upper, or warm side, of the insulation. Insulation should also be provided on any basement wall and access panel adjacent to the crawl space.

Where this approach is used, good cross ventilation should be provided, allowing at least a square foot of vent area for every 500 square feet of crawl space. This ventilation is maintained summer and winter.

If heating and plumbing supply lines run through an unheated crawl space, they should be insulated as well. This prevents heat loss from the ductwork and freezing in the plumbing. During the summer, this also helps minimize condensation. The vapor barrier on this insulation should be applied externally.

The second philosophy is to consider the crawl space as part of the house and heat it as such. This involves insulating the perimeter walls of the crawl space (to R-8 or R-12 as discussed in Chapter 8). The insulation can be added to the interior or exterior of the crawl space walls. The vapor barrier, if any is needed, again is applied on the warm side of the insulation. Heating the crawl space eliminates the need to insulate the heating and plumbing lines running through the area. However, ventilation and a vapor barrier over an earth floor are still required. The ventilation is kept open during the summer and blocked off (and insulated) during the winter.

Where no insulation is found in the crawl space, it is usually easiest to adopt the second technique and add insulation from the exterior.

SUMMARY

The major concern in a basement is usually moisture. In most cases, problems can be cured inexpensively by outdoor work. Where this is not the case, however, the solution may be very costly. It is sometimes necessary to excavate around the entire perimeter of the building and add drainage tile—one of the most expensive home repairs.

In areas with a high-water table, the chances of having a wet basement are greatly increased. Furthermore, the solution to the problem may be considerably more costly. Basement walls and floors are generally waterproofed rather than dampproofed. Any failure in the waterproofing usually necessitates digging. A sump pump system is often used to collect and discharge water standing outside the basement. This arrangement may be satisfactory if the problem is occasional and not too severe. However, where you find a sump pump and/or evidence of extensive moisture problems, it is best to investigate further. Professional building inspectors and municipal building officials may be able to help. Try to find out whether a high-water table does exist and, if so, whether it is a constant or intermittent condition. It may be wise to move very slowly on a house with this type of problem.

CHECKLIST—The Basement and Crawl Space

Signs of Moisture

1. Valuables stored directly on floor?

2. Paint peeling or water stains on walls?

3. Efflorescence on walls or floors?

4. Rust around furnaces, water heaters, laundry tubs, etc.?

5. Stained or rotted wood at floor level?

6. Rust around nail heads and electrical outlets near floor?

7. Wood subfloor springy?

8. Carpet musty?

9. Floor hollow below concrete?

Basement Windows

1. Evidence of leakage?

2. Wood rotted around frame?

3. Window well clean?

4. Good drainage?

5. Storm on window?

Exterior Basement Stairwell

1. Six-inch door threshold?

2. Drain in landing?

3. Railing on stairwell?

4. Condition of stairs and retaining wall?

General

1. Floor drain?

2. Floor slope toward drain?

3. Laundry tubs leak?

4. Electricity or gas for clothes dryer?

Sump Pump

1. Why present?

2. Condition?

3. Operable?

4. Discharges where?

Finished Basements

1. Height?

2. Windows?

3. Ventilation?

4. Exits?

Crawl Spaces

1. Structural problems: Rot?
                        Termites?

2. Foundations?

3. Access?

4. Insulation?

5. Ventilation?

6. Vapor barrier?

7

THE INTERIOR

On one hand, the interior finish of a house is one of the easiest items to inspect because it is something familiar. On the other hand, it is also one of the most difficult because it is very hard to remain objective. During the interior inspection, avoid thinking about owning the house or decorating it. The more detached you can remain during the inspection, the better off you will be in the long run.

Certain components of interiors are common to all rooms. In the following pages, these will be discussed generally; however, each component should be inspected in every room. Specific items found in only one or two rooms, or specialty rooms, will be discussed at the end of this chapter.

WALL AND CEILING FINISHES

A careful examination should be made of all the interior wall and ceiling finishes throughout the house. Interior wall finishes are normally made of plaster over some type of lath, or drywall. It is sometimes difficult to determine which is which in a finished home. Generally, houses

FIGURE 7.1 *Gypsum Lath versus Drywall*

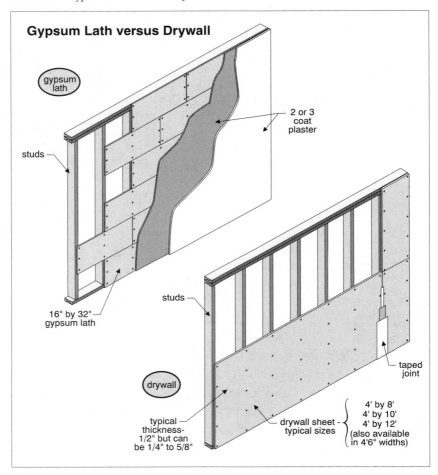

Gypsum Lath versus Drywall

gypsum lath

2 or 3 coat plaster

studs

16" by 32" gypsum lath

studs

taped joint

drywall

typical thickness- 1/2" but can be 1/4" to 5/8"

drywall sheet - typical sizes

4' by 8'
4' by 10'
4' by 12'
(also available in 4'6" widths)

built before 1950 or 1955 are plaster, while homes newer than this are drywall. However, there are many exceptions.

Plaster walls consist of several components. The first is the lath (a base for the plaster), which is fastened to the wall studs, or wall strapping in the case of a solid masonry wall. The lath can be wood, metal, or gypsum board panels (see Figure 7.1). The plaster covering itself is applied in two or three layers. Plaster usually consists of a mixture of gypsum, sand, and water. Plaster walls are sometimes thicker than walls made of drywall; one-half of an inch is a common thickness. Plaster walls, including the lath, are structurally more rigid than walls made of drywall and tend to be more soundproof.

Minor cracks or damage to plaster walls should not be a major concern; however, walls and ceilings should be inspected carefully for plaster separating from the lath below. This will create a bulging or spongy surface. Repairs to this type of wall surface can be costly.

Drywall, or plaster board as it is commonly known, is essentially a manufactured plaster wall with a paper finish. It is available in sheets of various sizes and thicknesses. Sheets are typically four feet wide and come in common lengths of eight, ten, and twelve feet. The most common thicknesses of drywall are three-eighths, one-half, and five-eighths of an inch. Three-eighths drywall is commonly used for resurfacing existing damaged walls. It is considered too thin to be used on its own. In standard house construction, one-half-inch drywall is used; five-eighths-inch drywall is usually reserved for more expensive construction. Drywall is sometimes glued, but generally it is fastened to wall studs and ceiling joists with special nails or screws. The edges of the panels are slightly tapered to create a depression at the joints. The joints then are filled with a compound and a paper tape. After painting, the seams should not be visible.

In new construction, a phenomenon known as *nail popping* is quite common (see Figure 7.2). This occurs when the lumber that is used in building walls and ceilings dries and shrinks, forcing the nail heads out. This is easily remedied and should not be a major concern; however, excessive nail popping throughout a house may indicate a lower-than-average quality construction. As with plaster walls, minor cracking at high-stress areas around windows and doors is usual and should not be considered serious.

Acoustic ceiling tiles of various dimensions are commonly found on the ceilings of older homes and in finished basements. These materials are typically installed by home handymen who lack the expertise to drywall or plaster properly. On ceilings of older homes, tiles usually indicate a deteriorated plaster ceiling above, or an attempt to lower the ceiling height for whatever reason (some people feel that high ceilings waste too much heat, while others lowered their ceilings in an attempt to modernize their homes).

Inexpensive wood paneling is also normally installed by the home handyman, as well as by the large-scale development builder. Often the paneling is very thin. If this is the case, it should be installed over dry-

FIGURE 7.2 *Nail Pop Mechanism*

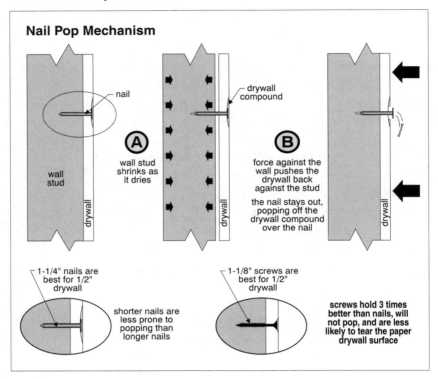

Nail Pop Mechanism

wall stud

drywall

nail

(A) wall stud shrinks as it dries

drywall compound

(B) force against the wall pushes the drywall back against the stud

the nail stays out, popping off the drywall compound over the nail

drywall

drywall

1-1/4" nails are best for 1/2" drywall

shorter nails are less prone to popping than longer nails

1-1/8" screws are best for 1/2" drywall

screws hold 3 times better than nails, will not pop, and are less likely to tear the paper drywall surface

wall or plaster. Frequently it is not. Push firmly on the wall between stud spaces to determine if some type of backing material has been provided.

During your inspection of walls and ceilings, look for stains and try to determine the origin of the moisture. Stains are most commonly caused by roof leaks, plumbing leaks, or condensation. If staining or water damage is noted, try to determine whether the leakage is still active or the quality of the repair work.

Be sure to inspect the ceiling and wall finishes in all closets. Often, defects are repaired within various rooms, but not in closets. Sometimes more information can be gained about the history of the house from closet spaces than from anywhere else in the interior.

FLOORS

Floors should be carefully inspected with two thoughts in mind: the levelness of the floor and the floor covering.

Some people are more sensitive to unevenness than others. Whether this is something you normally notice or not, you should make a conscious effort to note how level floors are when you're walking across them. This is sometimes difficult, depending on the amount of furniture in the room and the floor finish. A deep-pile carpeted floor tends to look and feel more level than a hardwood or tile floor does (a trick commonly used by renovators). Most minor floor slopes do not indicate serious problems. They are a result of warpage, shrinkage, or minor settling of the floor system. Houses are like people; they sag in the middle when they get older. Generally, if the floor systems in the house all slope towards the center, or towards the midspan of the floor joists, this is not a serious problem. If the floor systems slope towards one side or one end of the house, however, this may indicate more serious structural problems. Take note of any major sloping of floors, and return to the floor level below to check for causes. Refer to Chapter 2 for a discussion of structural issues.

Wood floors often squeak. This can be caused by a poorly fastened subfloor or the result of slight movement of the hardwood finish. Squeaky floors are usually difficult to eliminate; sometimes, however, the subflooring can be resecured or shimmed from below. Shims are simply wedges that can be driven into the space between the subfloor and the floor joists to stiffen up the floor and prevent movement. If the squeaking is a result of loose hardwood flooring that is shifting slightly, the annoyance can sometimes be reduced by sprinkling a dry lubricant, such as talcum powder, onto the floor and working it into the joints. Squeaky floors generally do not indicate any structural problems and, except that they're annoying and inconvenient, they should not be a concern.

Hardwood flooring is generally considered a high-quality floor finish. Depending on the thickness of the flooring strips, a marred and stained hardwood floor can be sanded and refinished, often with excellent results. Clues to the thickness of a floor covering can often be picked up at cuts through the floor. Perhaps the easiest place to determine this is at heating registers. If you lift out the grille cover, you can often tell how thick the floor is. Hardwood floors in one or two areas

FIGURE 7.3 *Types of Subflooring*

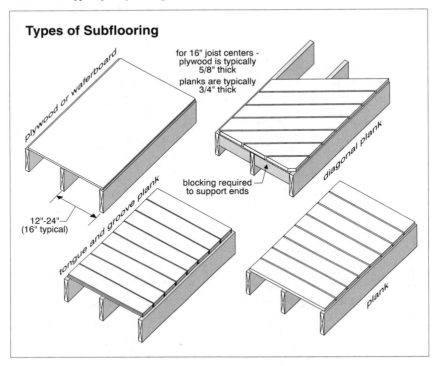

Types of Subflooring

plywood or waferboard

for 16" joist centers - plywood is typically 5/8" thick

planks are typically 3/4" thick

diagonal plank

blocking required to support ends

tongue and groove plank

12"-24" (16" typical)

plank

of a house do not indicate hardwood throughout. Often in older homes the first floor was hardwood while the upper floors had softer flooring, such as pine. In areas with wall-to-wall carpeting, do not assume there is hardwood below. Pick up clues wherever you can. Again, the floor registers are a good place to start.

Most exposed floor surfaces are installed over a subfloor. This subfloor can be made of plywood, chipboard, or softwood boards (see Figure 7.3). In most cases, the softwood subfloor was laid at right angles to the floor joists. The hardwood strips were then laid at right angles to the subfloor, which means the hardwood strips usually run in the same direction as the floor joists. Sometimes, this information can be valuable in trying to determine the framing of the house when analyzing structural problems. A note of caution here: Occasionally, the subflooring is installed diagonally to increase the rigidity of the house and to allow hardwood strip flooring to be laid in either direction. If the basement is unfinished, this can be determined from below.

Carpeting as well as resilient floor tiles or sheets can vary in quality dramatically. Look for obvious signs of wear in high-traffic areas.

WINDOWS

There are many different styles of windows installed in homes (see Figure 7.4). Unfortunately, quality varies as much as style. We will discuss some of the common window types, dealing with the materials typically used and the problems associated with each.

Single- and Double-Hung Windows

These traditional windows consist of sashes that move vertically in their frames. When closed, the inner window occupies the lower half of the frame and the outer window the upper half. When both the top and bottom sashes can open, this is a double-hung window. Only the bottom half opens on a single-hung window.

Locking hardware joins the top of the lower sash to the bottom of the upper sash. When opened, the windows are held in place by a counterweight and sash cord system, a spring-type guide, or simply a friction hold.

The window sashes and frames may be wood, aluminum, steel, vinyl, or a combination of materials. Unless they are well-weatherstripped, double-hung windows can be loose systems, and unless the glass is double-glazed (two panes of glass with an air space between), they require storm windows. The typically broad outer sills should be properly sloped to allow rainwater to drain away from the window. Incorrect sloping will trap water and may damage the sill and the wall system below.

It is not unusual to find these windows rendered inoperable by a number of coats of paint. The sash cord, pulley, and counterweight system that holds the window open is often nonfunctional because of broken sash cords or jammed pulleys (see Figure 7.5). When the sash cord is broken, the window can still be opened, but it must be propped up. Repairing old wood windows may take time and effort, but they are usually worth the trouble. If maintained properly, these windows can last the life of the house.

FIGURE 7.4 *Window Types*

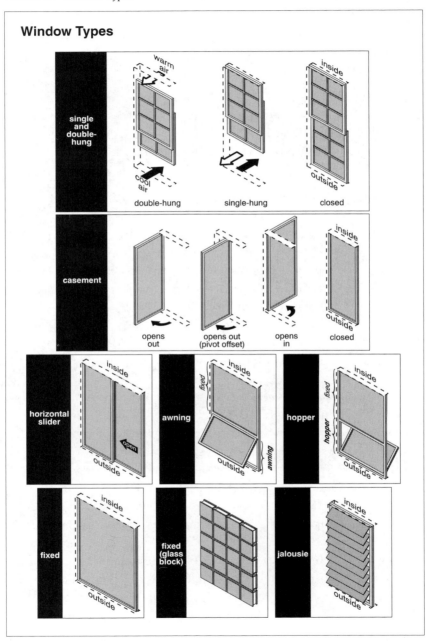

FIGURE 7.5 *Watch for Faulty Windows*

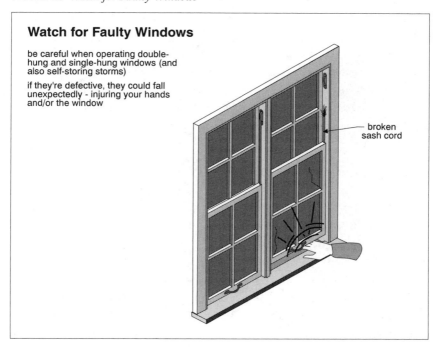

Watch for Faulty Windows

be careful when operating double-hung and single-hung windows (and also self-storing storms)

if they're defective, they could fall unexpectedly - injuring your hands and/or the window

broken sash cord

Casement Windows

Typically, these windows are hinged on one side and swing outward. Reverse casement windows are also side-hinged, but swing inward. They are usually operated by a crank or lever mechanism. Sashes are commonly made of wood, steel, or aluminum. Snugly fitting casement windows can be very weatherproof, but because of the casement windows swing, exterior storm windows and screens can be a problem. Storm windows are sometimes piggybacked onto the sashes, but this is a less-than-ideal arrangement. Usually, it is better to provide interior storms. Some modern casement windows can be opened on a pivot to facilitate cleaning both sides of the window from the inside.

Horizontal Sliders

These windows are common in new, modestly priced homes. The sashes and frames are often aluminum or vinyl, although wood is used on higher-quality windows. They have few moving parts and usually can be removed easily for cleaning. In some cases, the panes have no sashes and the glass rests directly on the guides. This type allows a good deal of air leakage. Horizontal sliding windows are usually installed with primaries, storm windows, and screens in three separate tracks. Many of these windows seem to be particularly susceptible to condensation problems. The bottom of the track should be provided with slots or holes to allow moisture to drain to the exterior. Proper drainage also includes an appropriate slope on the sill.

Awning Windows

This window is similar to a casement because it swings out, but it is hinged at the top. Reverse awning windows that swing inward are also available which swing inward. These are common installations in basements. Once again, they are operated typically by a crank or lever. Awning windows are often found below large, fixed picture windows and serve primarily as ventilators. Once again, fitting exterior storm windows is difficult and interior storms are generally considered preferable. Sash and frame materials are most often wood. Hopper windows are similar, except they are hinged at the bottom.

Fixed Windows

Fixed windows often take the form of large picture windows and provide additional light, but no ventilation. If located on a south wall, these windows can contribute to passive solar heating. The winter sun can add a good deal of warmth to a house as sunlight passes through large windows. Fixed windows, too, require storm windows unless they are double- or triple-glazed. Frames may be wood, vinyl, or metal. There is often no sash, with the glass resting directly on the frame.

It has become popular in some areas to renovate houses, removing the original double-hung windows and replacing them with fixed double-glazed windows. This eliminates the need for storm windows, screens, and operating hardware, but the house may be difficult to ventilate. Natural cross ventilation should be available at each floor level.

FIGURE 7.6 *Glazing Types*

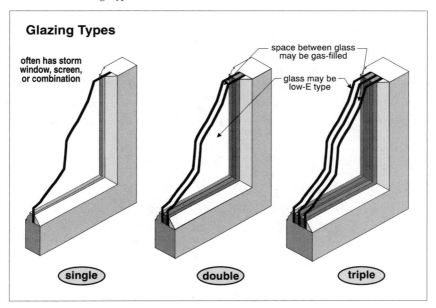

Glazing Types

often has storm window, screen, or combination

space between glass may be gas-filled

glass may be low-E type

single   double   triple

Jalousie Windows

These windows consist of many small awning windows, one overlapping the next in a vertical array. Several long, narrow panes of glass are laid horizontally in the frame, which is usually metal. When closed, the panes (which have no sashes) overlap each other. These windows are not weathertight and do not generally perform well in colder climates. They can, however, be a very effective means of obtaining good ventilation.

Double- and Triple-Glazed Windows

Glazing refers to the glass itself (see Figure 7.6). For instance, a double-glazed window is two panes of glass thick. Similarly, a triple-glazed window contains three panes of glass. The panes are separated by an air space. Double- or triple-glazed windows typically do not have storms. However, if they are the operable type, they must be provided with screens. On multiglazed windows, the screens are typically left in place year-round. In some high-quality installations, the screens are the roll-up type and can be hidden from sight.

The space between the panes of glass in some double- and triple-glazed windows is sealed, while in others the space is vented. The sealed type is very good in principle, but in practice the seal is difficult to maintain. When the seal is lost, condensation problems occur between the panes, and the window must be replaced. Very often a desiccant (drying agent) is installed when the window is manufactured. This helps reduce moisture problems on a small scale. To distinguish between the vented and sealed types, look for vent holes between the panes of glass.

Window Materials

Many different materials are used for window sashes and each has advantages. Wood sashes are reasonably good thermal insulators and do not generally contribute to condensation problems. They provide a sturdy sash and, if properly maintained, can last indefinitely. They are, however, susceptible to weathering damage on the exterior and if allowed to deteriorate are expensive to repair.

Metal sashes such as aluminum and steel are fairly durable if anodized or covered with a baked-on enamel finish, but if unprotected, both metals will oxidize. Metal window sashes are susceptible to condensation problems for they are good thermal conductors. In fact, these metals are several hundred times more thermally conductive than wood. Some metal sashes are thermally broken so that their conductivity is interrupted.

Vinyl sashes are fairly durable and usually do not require regular maintenance. They are also good thermal insulators (although not as good as wood). Their overall strength is somewhat less than that of some other sash materials. High-quality installations may employ a wood sash with a vinyl covering, thus enhancing the strength and durability of the wood with the low maintenance of the vinyl.

Storm Windows

Unless the primary windows are double- or triple-glazed, storm windows are generally considered necessary. There are two main benefits of a storm window: One is reducing air flow through gaps in the window system. The other is reducing heat loss through the glass. The dead air that is trapped between the two panes of glass acts as an insulator. However, the insulating value of storm windows is sometimes overstated. While a single-glazed window has a thermal resistance of approximately R-1, a single-glazed window plus storm will have a resistance of about R-2. Triple-glazing will result in an R value of approximately 3. When compared to a modern wall insulation standard of R-12 to R-20, the storm window provides little protection against heat loss in this fashion. Supposedly, triple-glazed windows on a retrofit basis have a payback period in excess of 15 years.

Storm windows do provide an additional seal, reducing air infiltration. In this way, heat loss is effectively reduced. One problem with exterior storm windows, however, is that they can provide too good a seal. When the seal on the storm window is tighter than the seal on the primary, the storm can be susceptible to condensation problems. In this situation, the warm moist air in the house leaks past the warm primary window and comes in contact with the colder surface of the storm. Because the temperature is much lower, the air's ability to retain its moisture is reduced and condensation forms on the cold storm surface. Both to prevent the storm seal from being too tight and to allow any condensation to drain to the exterior, many storm windows are provided with vent holes at the bottom.

Where interior storms are installed, similar problems can arise when an outer primary window fits more tightly than does an inner storm. In both cases, the problem can be overcome by improving the seal on the inner window or reducing the seal on the outer window.

Another advantage of using storms is higher inside humidity levels without condensation problems. Higher humidity levels during the winter months add to the comfort of the home. When the outside temperature is 0°F (-18°C), indoor humidity can be as high as 40 percent in a house with storm windows. When there are no storm windows, humidity levels as low as 15 percent can cause problems under the same conditions.

Older types of storm windows on the exterior have no screens and must be removed every spring and reinstalled every fall. This can be a big job on two- and three-story houses. For this reason, interior storms are generally considered more workable, unless a self-storing storm is used. A common type of self-storing storm is the aluminum combination storm. Typically, there is an upper and a lower pane of glass and a screen. The screen occupies the lower half of the window and one pane of glass occupies the upper half. The second pane of glass can be lowered to provide a continuous storm window or can be raised to allow air through the screened section.

Skylights

Skylights are popular additions to older houses. They can improve appearance, lighting, and even ventilation. They can be installed on flat or sloped roofs, and the panes can be glass or plastic. The plastic is highly resistant to breakage, but is susceptible to scratches. Skylights can be fixed or operable, with an opening skylight considerably more expensive. Single-, double-, and triple-glazed units are available, but only the latter two are satisfactory.

Skylight frames can be metal, wood, plastic, or a combination of these. Metal frames without a thermal break between the inner and outer surfaces can suffer condensation problems. These difficulties are aggravated by single-glazing and by placing a skylight in a room with high humidity, such as a bathroom.

Skylights have a reputation for leaking that is somewhat undeserved. Leaks are usually the result of a poor installation, and rarely a failure of the unit itself. Poor installations, however, are quite common, so look closely for evidence of leakage. Sometimes the seal between panes of the skylight will fail, resulting in condensation between the panes.

Inspection

In all cases, windows must be checked for operation. While replacing primary windows is often not necessary, the cost of repairs and rebuilding can be significant when you multiply the number of windows that need repair by the cost of the repairs.

On homes with single-glazed windows, storm windows are usually installed. Most of the older wooden storm windows have been replaced with aluminum units. These aluminum storms usually contain screens. Again, keep track of how many single-glazed windows are without storms. Providing a complete set of storm windows for a house is a costly project.

Where double- or triple-glazing is found, watch for condensation between the panes. This may mean the window will have to be replaced.

Look for evidence of leakage around skylights. This is very common on both flat- and sloped-roof installations. Also check to see that the skylight is at least double-glazed. Look for condensation problems both between and below the panes.

Check the hardware on all the windows. It is not uncommon to find it so badly covered with paint that the locking mechanisms do not work. Plastic hardware on less expensive windows tends to break off. Quite often much of the window hardware is broken or missing.

Examine the wall surface below windows. Sometimes windowsills are sloped incorrectly, resulting in water flowing down the inside wall surface and damaging it. This problem is most common at the corners of the windows so pull back the curtains and take a good look.

DOORS

Exterior doors should be solid or of panel construction. At least one exterior door should be large enough so moving large objects in and out of the house is possible. Both interior and exterior doors should be inspected for the quality of hardware.

Every door in the house should be opened and closed. Doorjambs should be checked for squareness. Even if the door fits properly, look carefully to see if the top or bottom of the door has been shaved to accommodate movement of the door frame. Doorjambs in partition walls tend to be more out of square than jambs in bearing walls are. Normally, bearing walls run at right angles to the floor joists. Most partition walls run parallel to the floor joists. Therefore, the entire weight of the partition wall rests on a single or doubled-up joist that tends to sag with age. As discussed earlier, this is not a serious problem; however, if a doorjamb in a bearing wall has moved significantly, this probably indicates a structural problem.

Many new homes have steel exterior doors. These doors are usually filled with insulation (see Figure 7.7). Normally, there are no problems with high-quality metal doors; however, metal doors tend to warp when the difference between inside and outside temperatures is extreme. The colder side of the door can contract while the warmer side expands, which causes the door to bow. Metal doors also present problems as the house settles. While it is relatively easy to shave a wooden door, modifying a metal door to compensate for movement of the door frame is more difficult. Many metal doors have plastic decorative trim fastened to the metal panels. With a good-quality storm door in place, and the sun shining on the door, the temperature build-up between the storm and the insulated metal door can be extreme. This can twist or warp the

FIGURE 7.7 *Door Cores*

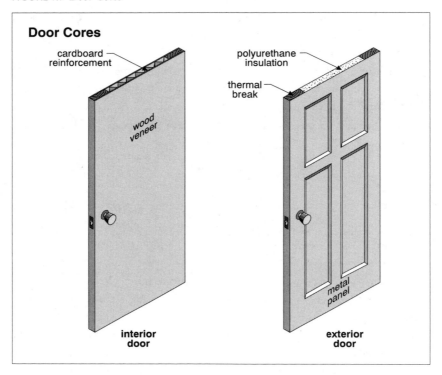

plastic trim and create an unsightly situation. Some metal door manufacturers do not recommend using storm doors in conjunction with their doors. Storm doors, however, on other types of exterior doors are a good idea.

ELECTRICAL CONNECTIONS IN ROOMS

While inspecting the interior of a house, note the electrical equipment within each room. Each room should have an adequate number of electrical outlets. Present standards call for outlets to be spaced so that one can be reached within six feet of any point on the wall. Many older homes and poorly renovated homes have a shortage of electrical outlets. If this is the case, remedying this situation can be expensive.

A small electrical tester that plugs into outlets can be purchased from most electrical supply stores. This tester will indicate whether the outlet is properly wired and grounded. It is not uncommon to find three-prong electrical outlets connected to older, two-conductor wire without a ground. In some rooms, this does not pose a serious problem for most of the electrical appliances that will be plugged in (lamps, clocks, etc.) do not have a ground pin. In kitchens, laundry areas, and work rooms, however, electrical outlets must be properly grounded. Computers and other home office equipment generally require grounded outlets as well.

Light switches should also be tested and overhead light fixtures should be noted and checked. The location of light switches is also important. Far too often, a switch is located on the wrong side of the doorway so that a person has to go around the door to use the switch. More details on electrical outlets, switches, and lights can be found in Chapter 3.

HEATING SOURCE

A heating source should be established within each room. Depending on the type of heating system used in the house, each room should be equipped with at least one supply air register, radiator, electric baseboard heater, or radiant heating panel. Ideally, heating supply units should be located on exterior walls below windows. With forced-air systems, note the number and location of return air ducts. In high-quality housing, a return air grille, or grilles, are located within each room. In older houses, and lower-quality houses, there are few return air grilles. In rooms such as bedrooms, where doors are commonly closed, there should be a one-inch space below the bottom of the door if no return air grille has been provided within the room. This will allow some movement of air throughout the home.

SPECIALTY FEATURES

Besides all of the components discussed previously that are commonly found in every room of the house, certain pieces of equipment are limited to one or two rooms.

FIGURE 7.8 *Masonry Fireplace Components*

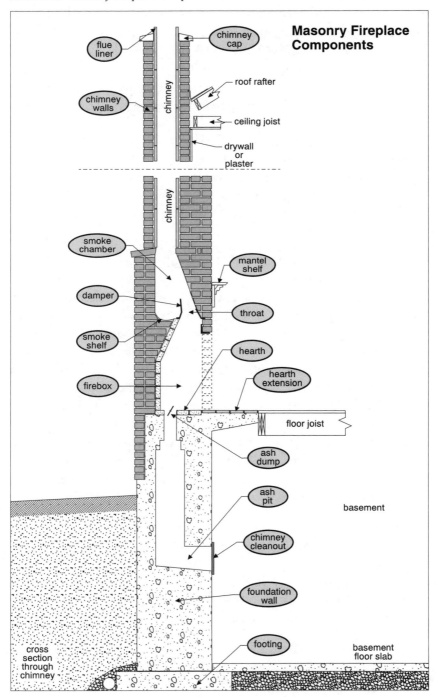

Masonry Fireplace
Components

flue liner

chimney cap

roof rafter

chimney walls

chimney

ceiling joist

drywall
or
plaster

chimney

smoke chamber

mantel shelf

damper

throat

smoke shelf

hearth

firebox

hearth extension

floor joist

ash dump

ash pit

basement

chimney cleanout

foundation wall

cross section through chimney

footing

basement floor slab

Fireplaces

Except for the relatively new, prefabricated fireplaces that are designed to collect heat from the fire and direct it into the house, most wood-burning fireplaces should not be considered a heat source. Because of their design, some fireplaces produce a negative amount of heat. In other words, more heat is taken from the house than is added.

When inspecting a fireplace, look for several things (see Figure 7.8). Fireplaces can smoke for several reasons. The size of the fireplace opening can be too large for the cross-sectional area of the flue; the proportions of the firebox itself can be wrong, or the chimney height and location can be incorrect, to name but a few. Proper fireplace design is too complicated a subject to deal with at any length in a book of this scope. However, one of the best ways to determine whether a fireplace will smoke or not is to look for smoke deposits on the front of the fireplace, under the mantle, or on the ceiling above. Even if a unit does smoke, relatively inexpensive methods of reducing or eliminating this problem are available. These include raising the level of the hearth to reduce the size of the opening for the fireplace, installing glass doors on the fireplace, or placing a draft cap on the top of the chimney.

Besides smoking fireplaces, other things should be considered. The firebrick in the firebox should be carefully inspected for cracked brick or missing mortar. Voids in this surface can create potential fire hazards. Look for an operable damper. Without a damper, a significant amount of heat can be lost through the unit.

Perhaps the most overlooked concern when inspecting fireplaces is an adequate number of flues. Chimneys can contain only one or several flues. A flue is simply a channel within the chimney. Only one major piece of equipment can be connected to each flue. Often, because of modifications within the house, or past building practices when the importance of one appliance per flue was not always recognized, two or more pieces of equipment were connected to a single flue. The most common situation is a two-flue chimney with a furnace connected to it in the basement, a fireplace connected to it on the first floor, and a second fireplace connected to it in the master bedroom immediately above. In this case, one of the two fireplaces should not be used for this will disrupt the proper performance of one of the other pieces of equipment. During an inspection, it is often difficult to determine which unit is connected to which flue. This will have to be determined

FIGURE 7.9 *Clearances for Unlisted Wood Stoves*

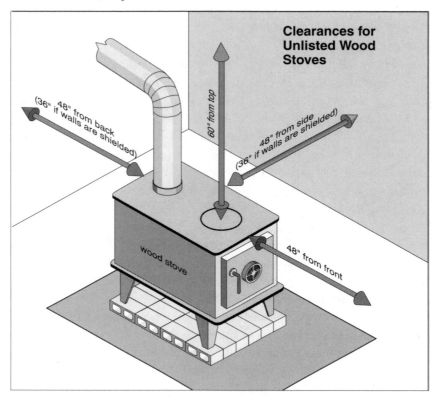

by more extensive testing at a later date. Obviously, one of the two fireplaces will be inoperable. Also check for the presence of a chimney. Some nonfunctional, decorative fireplaces look so authentic that it is easy to assume that they work. If there is no chimney within a reasonable distance of this fireplace on the exterior of the building, the fireplace is probably not connected to anything.

Wood stoves are often added to homes to supplement heating such areas as additions or basements. A wood stove can radiate a lot of heat, so it is important the stove is not close to combustible materials. Combustible materials can include stored firewood, furniture and wood floor, wall and ceiling framing. Drywall over wood wall studs is not enough to protect the wood from drying out to the point that it could burn. Very often, heat shields are needed to improve an existing installation. The proper clearances (see Figure 7.9) are usually noted on a data plate attached to the wood stove. If this information is not available, refer to local codes. It is not unusual for codes to specify a stove be placed a minimum of four feet from walls and five feet from ceilings. This is an important issue and should not be overlooked.

Gas fireplaces are common in many areas and can throw off a lot of heat. If the gas is turned on, be sure to test these fireplaces. A gas fireplace can be controlled by a wall switch, gas valve, thermostat, or remote control.

Staircases

Staircases should be carefully inspected for their structural integrity. Because the framing around the staircase is often the most difficult framing in the house, it is not uncommon for construction mistakes to be made that result in sagging staircases or stairs pulling away from walls. Look for signs of movement and try to determine the severity of any such movement. If the structural problem is not easily analyzed, bring in an expert. Check for a proper handrail (see Figure 7.10) and be prepared to install a handrail if one is not present. On more ornate staircases, carefully inspect the balusters (vertical spindles that hold up the railing) to ensure that they are all in place. Duplicating a broken or missing one can be an expensive proposition.

Closets

As mentioned previously, the condition of the interior finish within a closet can often provide a lot of information. In addition to possibly giving a history of the house's movement and any roof or plumbing leaks, one of the closets usually contains the access hatch to the attic. Besides their physical condition, the number and size of closets throughout the house should be noted. Many older houses lack closet space.

Kitchens

Kitchens should be thoroughly inspected for they are one of the most expensive rooms to redesign or refurbish. Generally, in this book we are concentrating more on the individual components of a house and on their condition rather than dealing with the arrangement of the house. In a kitchen, however, layout is paramount. This room must be large enough to accommodate your needs and it must work well. The

FIGURE 7.10 *Handrails and Guards*

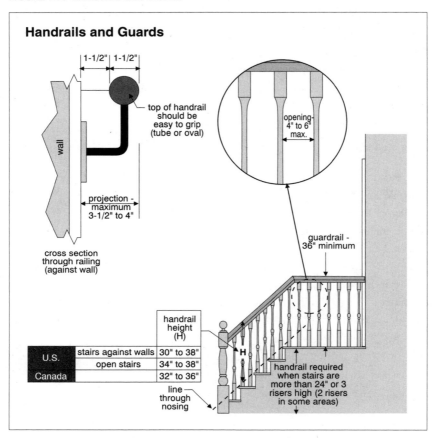

Handrails and Guards

		handrail height (H)
U.S.	stairs against walls	30" to 38"
	open stairs	34" to 38"
Canada		32" to 36"

1-1/2" 1-1/2"

top of handrail should be easy to grip (tube or oval)

opening 4" to 6" max.

wall

projection - maximum 3-1/2" to 4"

cross section through railing (against wall)

guardrail - 36" minimum

H

handrail required when stairs are more than 24" or 3 risers high (2 risers in some areas)

line through nosing

placement of the sink, stove, and refrigerator is critical. Ideally, these three items should be placed so that they form a triangle with an uninterrupted path from one corner to another. Besides the traffic flow within the kitchen, the location of the kitchen within the house is also important. A kitchen tends to be one of the focal points and therefore its proximity to the living room, dining room, and family room is very important.

If the appliances will be conveyed with the property, be sure to test them. The cost of a new stove and refrigerator is never a pleasant realization, but it is usually worse when it is combined with all the other costs of moving. The other major kitchen appliance to consider is a dishwasher. Is there one present? If not, is there room for one without sacri-

FIGURE 7.11 *Counter Problems*

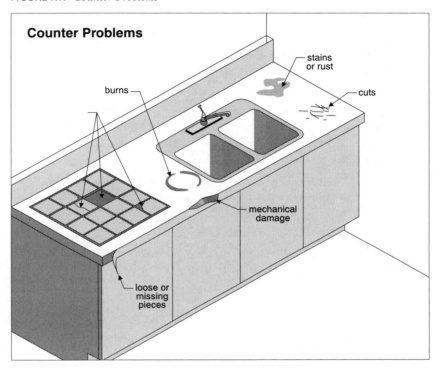

Counter Problems

- stains or rust
- burns
- cuts
- mechanical damage
- loose or missing pieces

ficing too much storage space? The amount of storage space and the quality of the cabinetry should be noted. Kitchen cabinets can be very expensive.

Water pressure should be checked in the kitchen. Also check the condition of the sink, the counters (see Figure 7.11), and the piping below, both supply and drainage. If a dishwasher is to be installed, it is best located near the sink. Will the present plumbing arrangement accommodate this?

Also note the presence of electrical outlets. In older homes, and even in some newer homes, there is a shortage of outlets. Outlets in the kitchen should be properly grounded, and in modern homes there may be ground fault interrupters. Ideally, these outlets should either be on 20-amp circuits or, where allowed, they should be "split" receptacles. This means that the upper receptacle on the outlet and the lower receptacle on the outlet are on separate circuits. This prevents excessive blowing of fuses. Outlets can be examined by removing the cover and checking the wire connections. If the small metal bridge, usually located on either side of the outlet joining the metal back plates behind each of the terminal screws, is broken and removed, the outlet has been split for there is no continuity between the top and bottom terminal on either side. To avoid an electrical shock, conduct this inspection with the power off, or have an electrician check this.

Also check for the presence of an exhaust fan above the stove or range top. There are two basic types: one that exhausts air to the outside and one that filters air through a charcoal unit and recirculates it. While fans that discharge air to the outside are less energy-efficient, they are still preferable to the other type. Fans that recirculate the air have a grille that is located near the top of the unit at the front and that blows the air back into the room. This type of fan is commonly found on an interior, rather than exterior, wall. Exhaust fans that vent to the exterior are usually found on exterior walls and a vent should be present on the outside of the house in the corresponding location.

Bathrooms

Besides the kitchen, bathrooms should also be inspected thoroughly. Determine the size, number, and location of bathrooms to see if they meet your needs. When you are inspecting a bathroom, look carefully for active or past leaks. Try to correlate these leaks with water stains or damage to ceilings and walls in rooms below. Leaks can originate in the supply piping itself, at the plumbing faucets, drainage piping, the connection of drainage piping to fixtures, and from overflows in bathtubs and sinks. If there is any question about the type of supply piping in the house, or the extent of its replacement, clues can often be picked up in the bathroom. Usually, the piping itself is visible and, when it is not, obvious repairs to tile and plaster work may indicate replacement. Thoroughly inspect and test every fixture in each bathroom. Sinks should be examined for chips, cracks, or stains. Test the sink faucets for leakage and proper operation. Water pressure should be checked, as discussed in Chapter 4. The cupboard doors below the sink should be opened to expose the plumbing while the faucets are running. Check to ensure that the sink drains properly, the waste plumbing does not leak, there is a proper overflow on the sink, and that there is proper venting to prevent siphoning of water out of the trap. Sometimes the presence of proper venting is hard to determine. Be more suspicious of S traps than P traps. These traps derive their

FIGURE 7.12 *Inspecting a Bathtub*

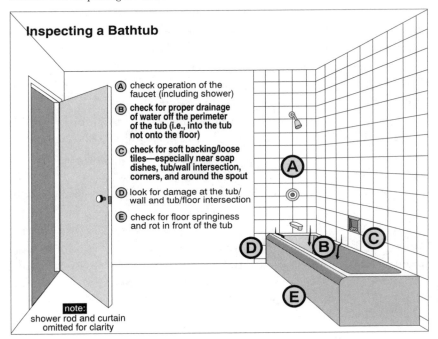

name from their shapes, which closely resemble the letter they are named after. While there is no surefire way to inspect venting once the interior finish has been installed, listen for siphoning and gurgling noises when all the water is drained rapidly out of a full sink.

Bathtubs should be inspected for chips, stains, and cracks (see Figure 7.12). Deep scratches or badly worn bathtubs, regardless of the material of which they are made, will present constant cleaning problems. They should also be inspected to ensure that they are properly secured to the walls and that they slope properly so that water landing on the upper ledges will not run out of the tub and onto the floor. Caulking around the edge of the tub should be in good condition and, if not, look for evidence of leaking. Faucets should function properly and should be turned on in conjunction with the faucets at the sink when determining water pressure. The bathtub should drain quickly. If it doesn't, either the drainage pipes are clogged or the design is poor. If the bathtub is used in conjunction with a shower head, the shower facility should be tested as well. The material around the bathtub should be suitably designed for a wet environment. All the tile in the bathroom, particularly the tile around the bathtub, should be carefully inspected for loose, cracked, or missing tiles. The grout between the tiles should also be in good condition. Many newer installations use one-, two-, or three-piece plastic enclosures. Grout joints are not an issue with these enclosures, but with any type of wall, the condition of the caulking around the edges is critical. Check the caulking at all the edges of the walls and at the points where the faucets protrude through the wall.

Glass doors on bathtubs or shower enclosures should be safety glass or plastic, should open and close easily, and should provide a good, watertight seal. The rubber strip at the bottom of a shower door is often damaged or missing completely.

Shower stalls, particularly if they are entirely tiled, are often prone to water leakage. This leakage sometimes occurs at the connection of the drain to the floor as well as at the seams between the walls and the floor. It is usually impossible to determine what type of shower pan has been installed underneath a tile floor; however, excessive caulking around any of the seams in the shower stall may indicate leakage problems. Light fixtures in shower stalls should be properly designed for use in a damp environment.

Toilets often leak at the seal between the toilet bowl and the floor. A toilet that can be rocked slightly from side to side may have a damaged or deformed seal (see Figure 7.13). While this is not an insurmountable problem, leakage over a long period of time can cause significant rot to the floor in this area. Constant condensation problems on the outside of the tank can do the same. In addition to checking that the toilet is securely mounted to the floor, also make sure that the tank is securely fixed to the bowl. Toilets should be carefully inspected for cracks, and the flushing mechanism and float valve should be checked to ensure proper operation. Usually, these mechanisms are relatively easy to repair or replace. While looking inside the tank, check for a manufacturer's date. This is usually located on the tank near the water line or on the underside of the lid. If you are reasonably sure that this toilet is the original fixture, this date will help establish the age of the house.

Another important feature in a bathroom is an exhaust fan. While an exhaust fan is not required when there is a window, a fan always helps to eliminate odors and reduce humidity within the room. High humidity leads to condensation problems that, in turn, can lead to rot. If there is an exhaust fan in the bathroom, be sure it discharges to the outdoors.

FIGURE 7.13 *Loose Toilet*

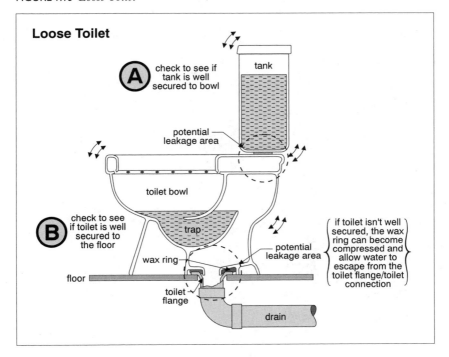

Loose Toilet

(A) check to see if tank is well secured to bowl

tank

potential leakage area

toilet bowl

(B) check to see if toilet is well secured to the floor

trap

wax ring

floor

toilet flange

potential leakage area

if toilet isn't well secured, the wax ring can become compressed and allow water to escape from the toilet flange/toilet connection

drain

An exhaust fan discharging into an attic space can create severe condensation problems in the attic.

You may feel somewhat embarrassed poking around under sinks and flushing toilets, but keep in mind that a house is a large investment and you have a right to know how well its major components function.

SUMMARY

Although you may find numerous minor deficiencies during your inspection of the interior, do not be too alarmed. Repairs to walls, floors, and ceilings are usually cosmetic in nature and are not expensive. Do not worry too much about specifics, but look for trends indicating poor workmanship. If what you can see has been poorly done, odds are that what you can't see has been done in a similar fashion. Concentrate on bathrooms, the kitchen, and windows. These are the most expensive areas of the interior.

CHECKLIST—The Interior

Walls and Ceilings

1. Structural cracks?

2. Cosmetic cracks?

3. Plaster: Spongy?
                Bulging?
                Pulling away from lath?

4. Moisture damage?

5. Nail popping on drywall?

6. Ceilings lowered?

7. Wood paneling: Thin?
                     Poorly supported?

Floors

1. Sloping?

2. Sagging?

3. Springy?

4. Squeaky?

5. Condition of finish on floor material? (Especially in high-traffic areas)

Windows

1. Type?

2. Operable?

3. Storms?

4. Double- or triple-glazed?

5. Sash and frame condition?

6. Glass condition?

7. Hardware?

8. Leakage?

9. Condensation?

Skylights

1. Plastic?

2. Scratched?

3. Condensation?

4. Leakage?

Doors

1. Operable?

2. Hardware?

3. Jambs square (evidence of settling)?

Electrical

1. Number and location of outlets per room?

2. Operable?

3. Overhead light fixture?

Heating Source

1. Register or radiator in each room?

2. Return air grilles: Number?
                        Location?

Fireplaces

1. Separate chimney flue?

2. Smoke on mantel or ceiling above fireplace?

3. Condition of firebox?

4. Damper: Inoperable?
                Operable?

Staircases

1. Sagging?

2. Pulling away from walls?

3. Damaged stairs?

4. Handrail? Condition?

5. Balusters? Condition?

Closets

1. Wall and ceiling cracks?

2. Water damage?

3. Door operable?

4. Hardware?

5. Size?

6. Number?

7. Attic access hatch?

Kitchens

1. Work triangle? (Sink, stove, refrigerator)

2. Adequate work area?

3. Condition of counters?

4. Adequate cupboard space?

5. Condition of cupboards?

6. Traffic flow?

7. Condition of appliances? (If conveyed with property)

8. Sink: Water pressure?
                Leakage below?

9. Adequate electrical outlets above counters?

10. Split receptacles?

11. Exhaust fan: Discharged to exterior?
                 Recirculating type?
                 Operable?

Bathrooms

1. Size?

2. Number?

3. Location?

4. Contributing to water stains below?

5. Evidence of pipe changeover from galvanized to copper?

6. Fixtures operable?

7. Electrical outlet?

8. Exhaust fan: Operable?
                   Discharging to exterior?

9. Water pressure?

10. Drainage?

11. Leakage below fixtures?

12. Shower head: Present?
                 Operable?

13. Condition of joint between bathtub and tile?

8

THE INSULATION

Home insulation has become more important with rising energy costs and the questionable reliability of energy supplies. Regardless of the energy source for the house—oil, natural gas, or electricity—a well-insulated home will be less expensive to heat and more comfortable to live in.

A brief discussion of how heat is lost should be helpful in understanding insulation. Heat can be transferred in three ways: conduction, convection, and radiation. *Conduction* is the direct transfer of heat between two bodies touching each other. For example, when you pick up an ice cube, your hand becomes cold. Heat is flowing from your hand to the ice by conduction. *Convection* is the transfer of heat by air movement. Consider a pocket of air that is warm. This air is lighter than the cool air around it, so it will rise carrying its heat with it. By convection, heat is moved from one location to another. This is why warm air in a house tries to escape through the attic, taking with it the warmth in the house. *Radiation* is the movement of heat by waves. One body can radiate heat to another without touching it and without air transporting the heat. The sun warming the earth is one example of this. An oven broiler cooking a steak is another example.

Insulation is designed to minimize the transfer of heat. All insulating materials take advantage of one special property that air has: Air is a poor thermal conductor (and conversely a good thermal insulator). Heat loss through air by conduction is very small. There is a problem, however. Air is very good at moving heat by convection. Insulation prevents air from doing this by trapping the air in little pockets and holding it in place. This is why insulating materials are very light; they are made up largely of small air pockets.

One problem still remains. As discussed, heat can radiate through air quite easily. Insulation, then, also has to provide a barrier against radiation. In general, the materials that prevent light radiation also prevent heat radiation. Prevention of heat loss by radiation is thus accomplished by using the solid materials that make up the insulation.

INSULATING VALUES

Generally, the thicker the insulation, the better it can do its job. This is, of course, because more air is held in place. However, we can also compare the performance of equal thicknesses of different insulations. The performance indicator used is the *R-value* of the insulation. This is a measure of the material's resistance to heat transfer, or its thermal resistance (see Figure 8.1). For example, one inch of a given type of insulation has an R-value of approximately 3. Thus, six inches of insulation would provide a total R-value of 18. Another insulation may have an R-value of 5 per inch. Six inches of this material would yield an insulation value of R-30. We can see, then, that some materials are more effective insulators than others. Several types of insulation and their insulating value per inch are detailed in the chart later in this chapter.

FORMS OF INSULATION

Insulations come in different forms, each with applications to which they are best suited. The four basic forms are loose-fill insulation (which can be poured or blown), batt or blanket-type insulation, rigid board, and foamed-in-place insulation (see Figure 8.2).

Loose-fill insulation is good for getting into small or irregularly shaped areas. It can also be blown or poured into wall cavities where

FIGURE 8.1 *R-Value per Inch*

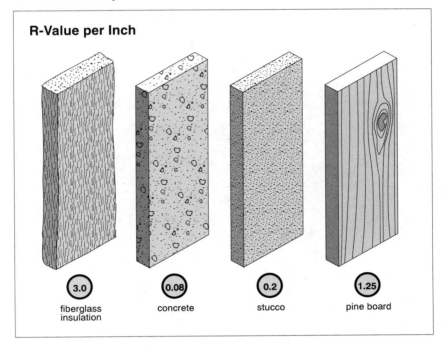

R-Value per Inch

| 3.0 | 0.08 | 0.2 | 1.25 |
| fiberglass insulation | concrete | stucco | pine board |

gravity will carry it throughout the coverage area. Loose-fill insulation is often installed by the homeowner. A separate vapor barrier must be provided.

The batt or blanket-form of insulation is relatively easy to handle and can be installed between wall studs during new construction or laid between ceiling joists in an existing attic space. This material, too, can be easily installed by the homeowner when adequate working space is available.

Rigid board insulation has some structural strength and is commonly applied on exterior wall or roof surfaces just underneath the siding or roof membrane. This board-type insulation can also be useful on basement walls where a wallboard or paneling can be applied directly to the insulation surface without wood framing. Some types of this board insulation are highly moisture-resistant and can be used on exterior walls below grade. No vapor barrier is needed with most rigid board insulations.

The foamed-in-place insulations are used where access is difficult. Holes are drilled into the wall and a liquid is mixed and blown into the

FIGURE 8.2 *Forms of Insulation*

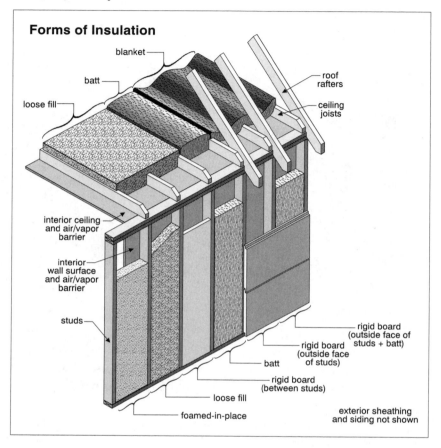

Forms of Insulation

cavity, then a chemical reaction creates a foam that hardens in place, filling the cavity. Generally considered a last resort, this method is usually expensive, and the number of homes with foamed-in-place insulation is relatively small. One type of insulation that was commonly used for this application was Urea Formaldehyde Foam Insulation (UFFI). The sale of UFFI was prohibited in the United States in 1982, but the law was struck down in 1983. UFFI was banned in Canada in 1980 and the ban still stands today. The controversy resulted from suspicions that health problems may be associated with the insulation. Modern evidence suggests that, in fact, no health risks are inherent in UFFI-insulated homes. A stigma still surrounds urea formaldehyde, which may have an effect on property values. The presence of this insulation is often difficult to verify. Testing laboratories will perform examinations to identify this insulation material. Many real estate transactions include clauses addressing this particular problem.

TYPES OF INSULATION

Each type of insulation has advantages and disadvantages. The ideal insulator would possess a high R-value per inch, and it would be completely resistant to moisture, fire, mildew, fungus, and vermin. It would be easy to work with and would pose no health hazard or discomfort. Its life expectancy would be indefinite. Needless to say, none of the insulation materials available has all of these properties.

Glass fiber insulation is one of the most common types available and is made from threads of glass. It is available in batt or blanket form as well as in loose fill. It is a fairly good insulator, but if compressed, it loses a good deal of its insulating value. It is resistant to moisture, mildew, fungus, and vermin, and is generally considered noncombustible. It is, however, a skin irritant, and inhaling small shreds of glass fiber can be dangerous.

Mineral fiber is similar to glass fiber except that rock or slag is used to form the wool-like texture. Its insulating value is comparable to glass fiber and it is similarly resistant to fire and rot. Furthermore, it is less irritating to work with than glass fiber is. Again, this material is susceptible to compaction, if loaded.

Cellulose fiber is essentially paper, finely shredded, that is treated with chemicals to make it somewhat resistant to moisture, fire, rot, and vermin. It is usually blown, but can also be poured or batts. Because of its relatively low cost, this material is very popular at present. Cellulose fiber is less prone to compacting than some of the other loose fill types, but it will absorb water, which will lead to deterioration.

Vermiculite is a mineral substance made from mica. This insulation is available as loose fill and can often be identified by the small rectangular shape of the individual pieces. Vermiculite is relatively expensive and is subject to damage by moisture. It is, however, noncombustible. Some vermiculite contains asbestos, so take care when disturbing this type of insulation.

Wood shavings or wood wool insulation should be treated with fire-retardant chemicals and can be made moisture-resistant. Where readily available, this insulation often provides good value.

Polystyrene insulation poses a fire hazard and should not be exposed to the building interior. This is available in board form or as loose fill. If applied on interior walls or ceilings, it should be covered with at least one-half-inch drywall or plaster. While this material has a good R-value per inch of thickness, it is often somewhat more expensive than other types. No vapor barrier is required with the rigid boards. Extruded polystyrene has a smooth appearance to it, while expanded polystyrene is made up of little beads.

Isocyanate, polyisocyanate, and polyicynene are foamed-in-place insulations that are often used in new construction to fill wall and floor cavities before interior or exterior finishes are applied. These materials cannot be blown into existing, enclosed cavities.

Foamed-in-place urea formaldehyde foam insulation is no longer in common use, as discussed previously. This insulation is used in other countries, but at present it is a controversial material.

Phenolic foam board is a good insulator and is highly resistant to most of the enemies of insulation that were discussed. It has the disadvantage of being somewhat expensive. A separate vapor barrier is required.

Different insulations, then, are best suited for different jobs. Factors considered in the application of insulation are R-value, cost, ease of application, and health hazards, as well as resistance to water, fire, mildew, fungus, and vermin. In some cases, structural integrity is desirable.

AMOUNTS OF INSULATION

The amount of insulation that is required depends, of course, on the climate. The values mentioned here (see Figure 8.3) apply to the northern half of North America. Local building authorities can tell you what is required in your area.

Unheated attic spaces should be insulated to between R-25 and R-40. The insulation is typically applied directly over the attic floor.

In most houses, there is no need to heat the attic area and its temperature should approach the outdoor temperature. Where vertical wall surfaces are in a roof or attic space, and one side is heated, an insulation value of approximately R-20 is recommended.

FIGURE 8.3 *Recommended Insulation Levels*

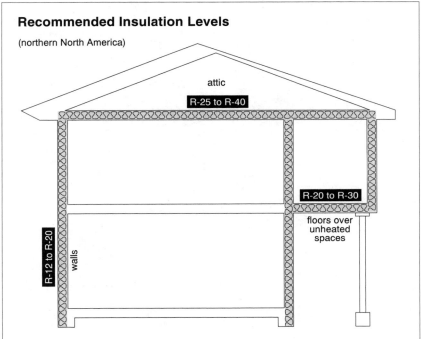

Where no attic exists and the room ceiling is also the roof line, insulation values of R-20 are recommended. Roughly R-20 to R-30 valued insulation is applicable for floors over unheated porches or garages.

Exterior wall insulation should be at least R-12. In new houses this insulation is often R-20.

Basement wall insulation should be at least R-8 if more than half of the basement is below grade. The insulation should be at least R-12 (treated then as a normal exterior wall) if more than half of the basement is above grade.

Where a crawl space is to be heated, the perimeter walls of the crawl space should be insulated to at least R-8. Again, if more than half of the crawl space is above grade, R-12 would be appropriate. Where a crawl space is to remain unheated, the floor of the room above should be insulated to approximately R-26.

The construction materials used in exterior walls have some insulating value, but it is surprisingly low. For example, one brick has an R-value of less than 0.5. A four-inch concrete block has an R-value of 0.75.

FIGURE 8.4 *Vapor Barrier Location*

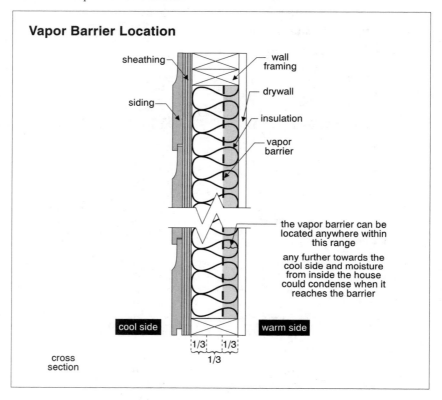

Vapor Barrier Location

sheathing

siding

wall framing

drywall

insulation

vapor barrier

the vapor barrier can be located anywhere within this range

any further towards the cool side and moisture from inside the house could condense when it reaches the barrier

cool side

warm side

1/3 1/3

1/3

cross section

Exterior sheathing is worth about R-1.0 to R-1.5. An uninsulated air space between two-by-four-inch studs in a frame wall has an R-value of less than 1.0. A ½-inch-thick drywall panel (gypsum board) provides approximately R-0.3.

Uninsulated wood-frame or masonry wall systems have R-values ranging between 3 and 5 for the most part. When compared with the recommended minimum value of R-12 for an exterior wall, the need for insulation becomes apparent.

VAPOR BARRIERS

A vapor barrier should always be provided on the warm side of insulation (see Figure 8.4). With the exception of some rigid insulation boards that are moistureproof, most insulation requires vapor barriers.

The vapor barrier is designed to prevent moisture inside the house from getting into the insulation and wall system. Moisture not only reduces the effectiveness of insulation (water is a good thermal conductor), but can also damage the building materials.

INSPECTION

When inspecting a house, try to identify the types of insulation used and, by noting the thickness, determine the R-value from this chart.

R-Values for Different Insulating Materials

Material	Approximate R-value per inch
Fiberglass (loose fill)	3.0
Fiberglass (batt)	3.2
Cellulose fiber (loose fill)	3.5
Mineral wool (loose fill)	3.1
Vermiculite (loose fill)	2.4
Expanded polystyrene board	4.0
Extruded polystyrene board	5.0
Polyurethane (foamed-in-place)	6.0
Isocyanate (foamed-in-place)	4.3
Wood shavings (loose fill)	2.4
Phenolic board	8.0

The Attic

The most important area to inspect for insulation is the attic, where heat loss can be the greatest. Attic insulation can usually be examined by viewing the attic from a hatch in a hall or closet on the level below. (A word of caution here: It's best to check with the owner first. In some cases, loose-fill insulation has been added from above and if the access hatch is opened, a good deal of insulation may end up in the room below.)

As discussed, the type and thickness of the insulation should be noted so you can calculate the R-value. Look for uneven or missing insulation. Also, check for insulation and weatherstripping on the access hatch cover.

Very often you will find two different types of insulation. For example, there may be three inches of original mineral wool covered by six inches of cellulose fiber. If this is the case, add the R-values for each layer of insulation together.

Where different types of insulation have been installed, there should be no vapor barrier between the two. This will trap moisture within the insulation. (If a vapor barrier is noted, it can be slashed to allow warm, moist air to pass through.) There should, however, be a vapor barrier below all of the insulation. This vapor barrier may be kraft paper fixed to the underside of the insulation batt, a sheet of clear plastic (polyethylene), tar paper, or aluminum foil. If no vapor barrier has been provided, it is difficult to lift up all the insulation and add one. An alternative solution is to cover the ceilings below with a paint designed specifically as a vapor barrier. Aluminum paints, marine varnishes, and oil-based paints will also work to some extent. It's helpful as well to caulk openings in ceilings from below to prevent moisture escaping into the attic.

While handling the insulation, you will have noticed whether or not it is damp. If so, it is important to ascertain the source of the dampness. It might be caused by condensation, a leak in the roof, or water backup due to ice damming. For a discussion of these problems, turn to Chapter 1.

Insulation should not cover any recessed light fixtures or exhaust fan motors. Heat can build up around these items, creating a fire hazard. Insulation should be kept three inches away from such fixtures.

Some houses have more than one attic and access should be gained to all of them if possible. A strong light is necessary to view the entire attic from the access hatch. It is usually not safe to walk in the attic space. It's very easy to put your foot through a plaster or drywalled ceiling—a stunt not likely to endear you to the owner of the house.

Where There Is No Attic

A house with a flat roof or a cathedral ceiling has no attic space. If this is the case and the house is old, chances are the roof cavity was never insulated. But if you notice plugs on the ceiling or on the roof covering, this probably means that insulation has been blown in. In most cases, though, you won't be able to check this insulation.

FIGURE 8.5 *Insulating Flat (and Cathedral) Roofs*

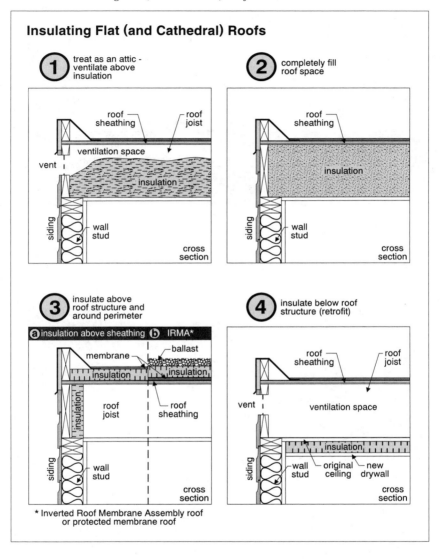

Insulating Flat (and Cathedral) Roofs

1 treat as an attic - ventilate above insulation

roof sheathing
roof joist
ventilation space
vent
insulation
siding
wall stud
cross section

2 completely fill roof space

roof sheathing
insulation
siding
wall stud
cross section

3 insulate above roof structure and around perimeter

ⓐ insulation above sheathing **ⓑ IRMA***

membrane
ballast
insulation
insulation
insulation
roof joist
roof sheathing
siding
wall stud
cross section

4 insulate below roof structure (retrofit)

roof sheathing
roof joist
vent
ventilation space
insulation
siding
wall stud
original ceiling
new drywall
cross section

* Inverted Roof Membrane Assembly roof or protected membrane roof

The most common method of upgrading a house with no attic is to blow insulation into the roof cavity (see Figure 8.5). This cavity is often not deep enough to add the recommended R-20 insulation and to leave adequate room above the venting. Even if there is sufficient space, it's almost impossible to introduce the insulation evenly, leaving a continuous vented area above.

FIGURE 8.6 *Evidence of Insulation Added*

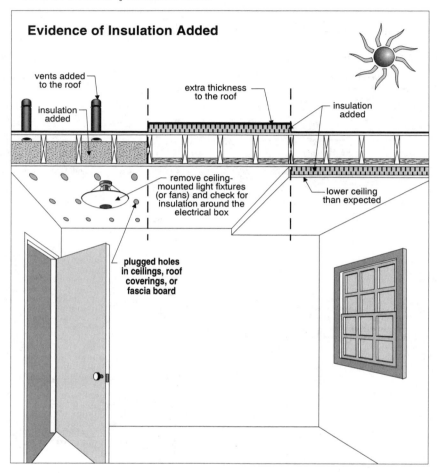

When homeowners retrofit a flat roof or cathedral ceiling, they sometimes sacrifice ventilation altogether and completely fill the roof cavity with insulation. In this situation, particular attention must be paid to establishing a good vapor barrier.

If the flat roof membrane must be replaced, it may be better to insulate above the roof boards (see Figure 8.6). Rigid board insulation is often used for this application. The old roof covering is removed, insulation is added, and a new roof membrane is installed. A variation of this approach involves putting the insulation above the roof covering and adding gravel on top. In either of these applications, the roof space between the ceiling and roof boards is heated and no ventilation should be provided.

Exterior Walls

Exterior wall insulation is difficult to check except around wall openings. Sometimes by removing the cover plates on electrical outlets or light switches, you can see the insulation. Care should be taken, however, that nothing inside the electrical box is touched. In solid masonry construction, there often is no wall insulation. Where two courses of brick are covered on the interior by wood strapping and lath and plaster, there is no room to provide insulation cost-effectively.

Basement Walls

Basement wall insulation can readily be examined in an unfinished basement. On new houses, insulation is sometimes found only down to two feet below grade level. It is often economical to add insulation all the way down to basement floor level. Where the basement walls are paneled, again, look carefully around wall openings and at electrical outlets. In some cases, basement wall insulation has been provided on the exterior of the house and may not be visible.

AIR LEAKAGE

One of the greatest causes of heat loss in many houses is air leakage. When a house is not well sealed, the cold winter air finds its way into the house. This infiltration of cold air can be greatly reduced by caulking (see Figure 8.7) and weatherstripping doors, windows, and other openings. This is an inexpensive and effective way to reduce heating costs.

SUMMARY

It is important to understand that many old houses will not be insulated to the levels recommended here. However, this is not a sufficient reason to reject an older house. In many areas, government grants are given to homeowners who upgrade their home insulation.

FIGURE 8.7 *Caulking–Indoors or Out?*

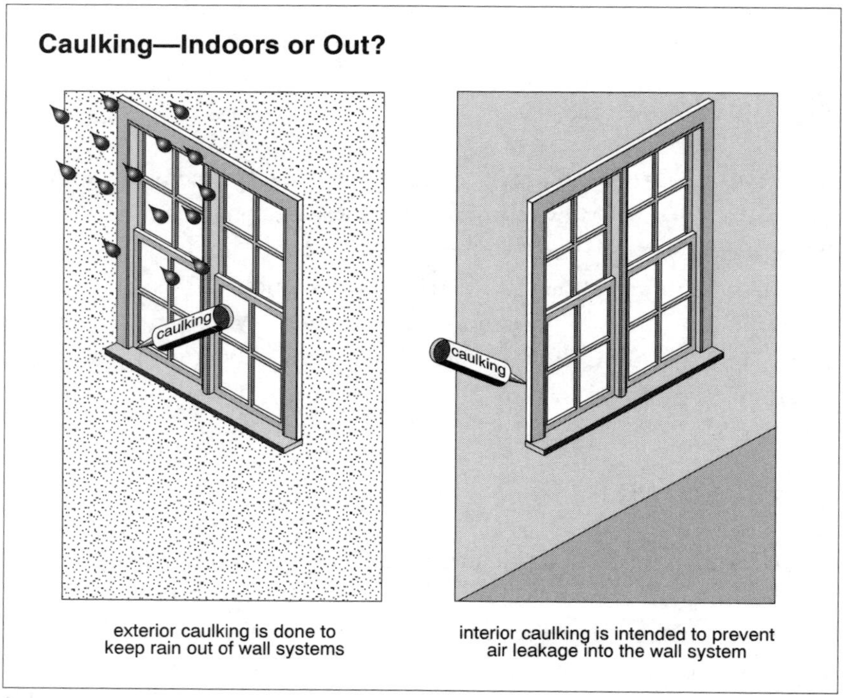
Caulking—Indoors or Out?
caulking
caulking
exterior caulking is done to keep rain out of wall systems
interior caulking is intended to prevent air leakage into the wall system

There is a limit, however, to how far one can practically upgrade insulation. The law of diminishing returns comes into play, and one should consider the payback period in reduced heating costs against the initial cost of installation. The presence or absence of insulation is not usually a determining factor in the buying decision.

CHECKLIST—The Insulation

1. Type?

2. Amount?

3. R-value?

4. Vapor barrier?

5. Ventilation?

9

THE ATTIC

Before you buy any house, you should inspect the attic very carefully. Some houses have more than one attic and access should be gained to all of them if possible. You can usually view the attic through a hatch in one of the second-floor closets. Remember to make sure the attic hasn't been insulated from above with loose-fill insulation (which will rain down on you when you open the hatch) and to bring a strong light with you.

INSULATION

For a complete discussion of attic insulation, turn to Chapter 8.

VENTILATION

Even where a vapor barrier has been provided under insulation, some moisture will enter the attic. With good ventilation, this moisture can be removed before it condenses. A well-ventilated attic will have openings at the top and bottom, allowing good air movement through-

FIGURE 9.1 *Recommended Amount of Attic Ventilation*

Recommended Amount of Attic Ventilation

the total vent area is often recommended to be 1/300 of the floor space of the attic

1 square foot of upper vent area required for 600 sq. ft. attic area

roof vent

note:
the actual vent opening must be larger than 1 sq. ft. because of screen/louver obstructions

roof rafter

air flow

insulation

ceiling joist

soffit vent

wall

1 square foot of lower vent area required for 600 sq. ft. attic area

cross section

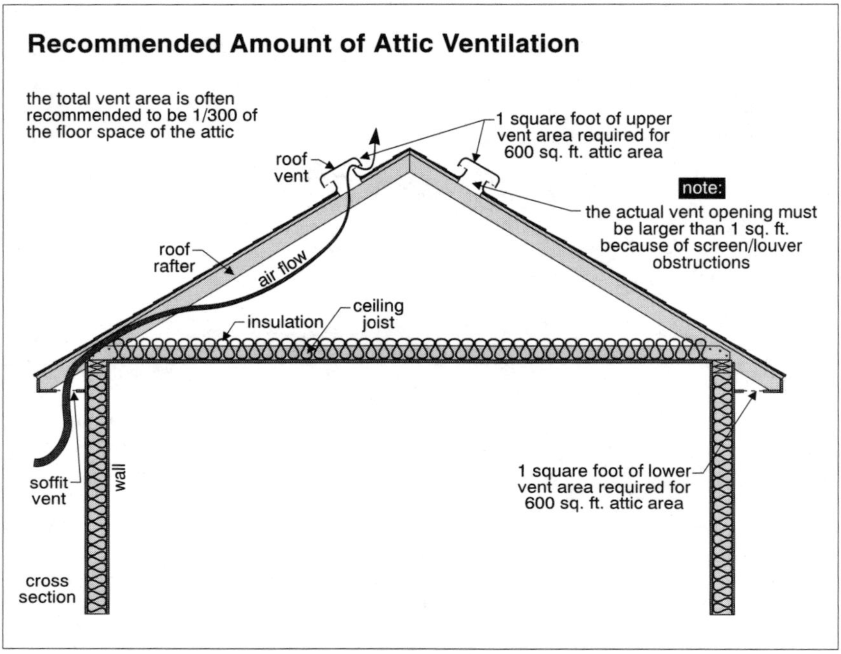

out the attic space (see Figure 9.1). Openings at the bottom are usually installed under the eaves and are called soffit vents. A continuous ridge vent may be provided along the peak, or dome-type vents may be installed near the top. In any case, all sections of the attic should be vented. There should be approximately 1 square foot of ventilating area for every 300 square feet of attic area. If the vents are screened, vent area should be increased to 1¼ square feet. If louvers are provided, there should be roughly 2 square feet of venting for every 300 square feet of attic space.

Some attics have exhaust fans that improve the ventilation. These fans may be controlled manually, by a thermostat, or by a humidistat. In principle, these fans are good, but in practice they seem to require a good deal of maintenance. Using these fans in the winter to reduce moisture in the attic is not recommended, for they may pull warm, moist air out of the house and increase heat loss. During summer months, these fans help to remove the warm attic air, thus keeping the house cooler. Even if there is no fan, a well-ventilated attic will help keep the house cooler during the summer.

Some attic fans also remove air directly from the house. This is accomplished by opening hatches in the ceiling and drawing warm air up out of the house. These fans are often very powerful and some precautions must be taken before operating them. The fireplace damper should be closed. If the damper is open, soot and ash may be drawn into the house from the chimney. Also, the furnace should not be operating. In some cases, the flame of a furnace burner has been drawn out of the firebox and has destroyed the burner assembly. It is even possible to draw furnace exhaust gases into the house, which is a serious threat to life safety. It is best not to operate these fans at all during the winter.

Where an attic fan is provided, loose-fill insulation may not be appropriate. The attic fan may be able to pick up the insulating material and exhaust it! It is best to provide an insulated cover for the fan during the winter.

Where vents are installed in gable end walls, look for birds' nests, beehives, and other obstructions that will restrict air flow. Check to see that screening on vents is intact to keep birds and animals out. Make sure soffit vents have not been covered with insulation. You should be able to see daylight at these vents.

VENTILATION WHERE THERE IS NO ATTIC

Good ventilation is more difficult to achieve in a house with a flat roof or a cathedral ceiling. Because there is less room in the roof space for air movement, the venting requirements are higher. Two square feet of ventilating area should be available for every 300 square feet of roof area. Vent areas should be increased to 2½ and 4½ square feet for screening and louvers, respectively. Unless provided on initial construction, it is difficult to achieve this ventilation between the insulation and the roof deck.

MOISTURE PROBLEMS IN ATTICS AND ROOF SPACES

To determine if there is excessive moisture in an attic, touch the insulation to see if it is damp. Look at the underside of the roof boards and rafters for the black discoloration that indicates mildew. Rust around roofing nails and other metal projections also indicates excessive moisture.

If there is a moisture problem, it will probably come from one of three sources. The first is condensation, most likely caused by poor ventilation. The second is a leak in the roof membrane. The third is water backup as a result of ice damming. (See Chapter 1.) By keeping in mind the ways in which water can enter an attic, you can determine the cause of the problem.

If condensation is the culprit, the moisture problems will be relatively uniform across the roof surface. Evidence of dampness, such as rusted nails and mildew, may be more pronounced near the peak and less noticeable near any vents.

Where leakage is the problem, water staining of the wood will be localized. Water may enter near the top and follow one or two rafters down to the ceiling, but it does not usually spread horizontally. Areas where leakage may be expected include chimney and plumbing vent penetrations, and at valleys and changes of roof direction.

Ice damming will result in water stains on the lower sections of the roof only. The problem is usually continuous along the length of the attic. If ice damming is the problem, woodwork on the eaves may also show some deterioration.

Moisture problems in houses where there are no attics are often difficult to trace. Evidence of problems within the roof space may show up as staining on the ceiling finish below. This may be most noticeable around light fixtures or around the heads of the nails holding the ceiling finish in place. Difficulties may also be indicated by a sagging ceiling. The cause may be leakage or condensation and it may be best to get some help from a specialist.

EXHAUST FANS

Where bathroom or kitchen exhaust fans have been noted in the house (see Figure 9.2), make sure they do not discharge their warm, moist air into the attic space. Exhaust ductwork should extend through walls or through the attic, directing the air to the outside. Where ducts are metallic and the distance through the attic space is several feet, it may be necessary to insulate the ductwork to prevent condensation from forming on the inside of the duct walls.

FIGURE 9.2 *Exhaust Fan Conditions*

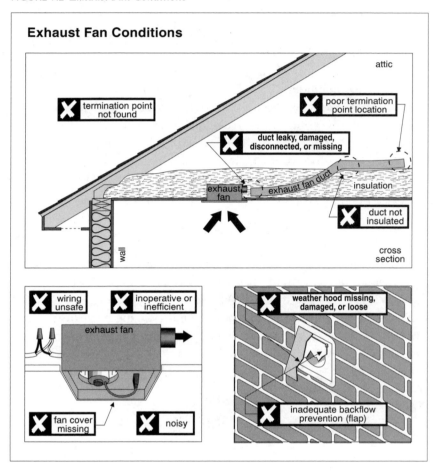

ROOF FRAMING

The roof framing should also be examined when you are in the attic. Look for sagging or cracking in the rafters. Depending on the size and shape of the roof, there may be collar ties (horizontal wood members secured to the midpoints of rafters on opposite sides of the roof). These keep the rafters from sagging. There may also be knee walls or dwarf walls to keep the rafters from sagging.

If the house was built during the past 30 years, the roof framing may be a truss system. A truss is a prefabricated wood triangle with diagonal and/or vertical bracing inside the triangle. The bottom of the truss forms the ceiling and the top two sides form the roof lines. Trusses allow greater spans for roofing systems, but do restrict storage areas. Trusses should not be cut to accommodate other building components, nor should the interior braces be removed.

Watch for rot or buckling of the roof boards. In older homes, these will be planks; in modern homes, plywood or waferboard is used. Where condensation problems have existed for some time, plywood roof sheathing may be coming apart (delaminating). Excessive moisture will destroy the glue holding the layers together and the integrity of the sheathing will be lost. If this situation is noted, expensive repairs may be necessary.

ELECTRICAL WIRING

Look carefully at any electrical wiring in the attic. Any wire connections should be made in metal junction boxes. It is not good practice to run wiring across the top of ceiling joists. If insulation is added, this wiring may be concealed from view. People walking in the attic or laying roof boards as a walkway may pinch the wiring and create a dangerous situation without realizing it. It is better to run the wiring through the ceiling joists.

SUMMARY

Most attic problems are moisture related, and once they are identified, they are not usually expensive to correct. If unattended, however, the resulting damage to interior finishes and structural members can be significant.

CHECKLIST—The Attic

1. Ventilation?

2. Attic exhaust fan operable?

3. Where do kitchen and bathroom exhaust fans discharge?

4. Evidence of moisture caused by condensation, leakage, or ice damming?

5. Framing condition?

6. Electrical wiring: Enclosed in boxes?
   Run on surface of joists?
   Recessed light fixtures kept free of insulation?

HOME RENOVATION

C h a p t e r

10

PLANNING A RENOVATION

Whether you are renovating your just-purchased house or the familiar home you've occupied for many years, the task can be daunting. Taking the time to carefully plan your home improvement project can mean the difference between a highly frustrating experience and a highly satisfying one.

ESTABLISHING A MASTER PLAN

With any home improvement, the most important steps are those taken before the physical work begins. The time to make your mistakes is while you are discussing the project around the kitchen table, or while the work is on paper. A disturbing number of projects get out of hand both from a cost and work-flow standpoint because changes or additions, caused by poor planning, are required during the renovation.

We recommend a problem-solving approach during the planning process. The first step is to identify all the problems in the house. What areas of the house simply don't work? Have each family member go through a day in his or her mind, trying to spot all the unsatisfactory situations. Deficiencies usually fall into four areas: a lack of space, a poor

181

layout with awkward traffic patterns, house systems in poor repair, and unsatisfactory aesthetics. Very often one problem is so prominent that others are not even considered until the project is completed. At that point, the second most serious problem becomes the major source of complaint. A well-planned renovation can solve many problems simultaneously. It is best to list the problems in order of priority. You may not be able to afford to cure all the ills in the first project, so this will help you decide where to trim if necessary.

When renovations are considered, one solution usually comes immediately to mind. You may think, We need another bedroom for the new baby. However, there are usually several possible solutions to any problem and the most obvious may not be the best. Remember, too, that there is generally more than one problem to be solved and we are looking for the best answer to the greatest number of problems. If a family is growing and another bedroom is needed, for example, perhaps the answer is a new master bedroom addition for the parents, with the baby taking over the existing room. If the original master bedroom is small, this solution will solve two problems simultaneously. It might even solve three problems if a second bathroom is added as part of the master bedroom suite. The important thing is to keep an open mind until all the possibilities have been considered.

When searching for more space, there are several ways to go. You can push walls outward, raise the roof, add a dormer, or finish an attic or basement area. Sometimes a room can even be found in existing living space that is currently wasted. Look in all directions for expansion possibilities.

When considering additions or renovations, it is tempting to picture the final product and concentrate on the interior finishes and furnishings. These, after all, are the areas that your guests will see and that will be the most admired. However, these are probably the least important areas of the project for they can (and probably will) be readily changed. It is much more difficult to get into the walls after the fact to upgrade the insulation, add an electrical outlet, or change the location of a heating register. The point here is to consider the basics before the cosmetics. Be sure the functional components make it possible to fully enjoy the new space. Many new bathrooms have to be broken up to replace old galvanized plumbing that should have been changed when the renovations were undertaken. Where funds are limited, it is probably best to compromise on finish (perhaps leaving some areas to be finished later) and to ensure you get all the space that you will need. The disruption of a major addition should only be experienced once in a lifetime.

Try to work the project to take best advantage of existing situations. For example, if you are opening up an attic and are going to include a bathroom, where should it be placed? It makes sense to line it up vertically with a bathroom immediately below, because there already is supply and waste plumbing up to that level. This type of thinking can save a good deal of money and time.

Because people change houses every four or five years, on average, it is wise to consider the improvements that add maximum value to your style of house, even if you have no intention of moving. Plans have a way of changing. Walk through the neighborhood, talk to your friends, consider what attracted you to the house, and determine what features are generally popular over the long term. Different areas have differing styles; local real estate agents can often provide good input about what improvements will add the most value.

If you do not plan to sell in the near future, be wary of fads. Many home improvements are popular for only a short time and may not add lasting value. Laundry chutes were considered a luxury for some time, but now that people are moving laundry facilities to the second floor, a chute may only be wasted space. In areas where rehabilitation is popular, sliding glass doors, for example, may be in vogue one year and wooden French doors the next. Generally speaking, the improvements that have the highest returns are modernized bathrooms and kitchens, or projects that add a bedroom, bathroom, or family room to the house. It is important that additions and improvements be consistent with the style and character of the home. For example, a Victorian-style house with a modern ranch-style addition will look somewhat odd.

Be wary of overimproving the property. Again, a real estate agent can help advise what renovations may be appropriate. While saunas and whirlpools may be quite suitable in one area, they may not add considerable value in others. Remember that location is paramount in real estate, and that the best house on the street will probably not command as high a price as it might deserve.

An old axiom is to buy the lowest-priced house and upgrade it. The return on your investment is usually greatest in this situation.

In summary, the planning stage is all-important, and a planning checklist is recommended, in which all existing components of the house are considered and possible changes to improve deficient areas are thoroughly investigated. This is the time to move slowly, talk to lots of people, look at the future, and, above all, remain flexible.

SETTING A BUDGET

Concurrent with the planning process, it is necessary to establish a budget figure. The most important thing is to decide how much you can afford to spend. Working from this figure, you can determine what kind of project to undertake. While this is difficult to do if you are unfamiliar with renovation costs, ballpark figures can be obtained from contractors and from neighbors and friends who have had similar work done. It is important to include all the costs involved. Remember that a major project may mean you have to move out of the house for a period of time. Consider the cost of relocation, hotel, or apartment expenses for a short time, or the carrying charges involved in temporarily owning two homes. Consider any interest charges on money borrowed, or the opportunity cost lost on moneys spent. Include building permit fees, fees required to have plans drawn up, insurance costs, property taxes, the fee for a survey of the property, any demolition costs, and storage costs for items such as furniture.

It is wise to leave a contingency for the unexpected. Very few projects come in under budget, and not a great many more make it exactly on budget. Furthermore, because you are dealing with an existing structure, there is usually some difficulty in matching new work to old. Additional costs sometimes become necessary when old wall finishes are torn down and deteriorated conditions are found inside. We recommend that a 5 percent slush fund be established. The temptation to avoid this is great, but consider it seriously.

Budgeting should not only be done with money, but with time as well. Particularly if you are interested in doing some of the work yourself, you must be realistic and determine exactly how much time you have to work on the project. Putting in a full day's work, then coming home to a do-it-yourself project while keeping a family together and maintaining any kind of a social life is a tall order. It is no wonder that construction debris is often referred to as "divorce dust." There are many "six-week projects" that are still under way two years after the starting date.

Even if the work is not performed by the homeowner, the project can be quite lengthy. For example, to add a second story to a bungalow, professionals will require at least three months to complete the project. This assumes a smooth work flow with no interruptions caused by weather, supply problems, strikes, etc.

Having set some type of realistic budget figure and having left a contingency, you must find a way to mesh the master plan with the budget. Unless you have considerable experience and confidence in your ability to estimate the cost of the project, it is wise to get some outside help.

MAKING THINGS HAPPEN

After you have established a plan that identifies the changes to be made, and after a budget is set, there are four general directions that can be taken. The first may be to engage an architect or a designer to provide assistance throughout the project. This consultant can get involved fairly early in the planning stages, follow through to the completed working drawings, help apply for permits, hire the contractors, and supervise the work. A consultant can also be engaged for any portion of this process.

The second alternative is to seek out a general contractor who may or may not be able to help with the design and the preparation of working drawings. He or she will usually take care of getting building permits and hiring and overseeing the subcontractors. He or she will also provide site supervision through the project.

The third option is to act as your own general contractor, hiring subcontractors at your discretion, and orchestrating their activities.

The last path is the do-it-yourself approach. In this case, the only outsiders involved in your project will be the municipal authorities who will have to approve your plans and inspect your work, and the suppliers who are providing you with materials.

Needless to say, there is room to work between these four distinct paths, and everyone must establish the correct blend for himself or herself. Each approach has its own advantages and disadvantages. Let's look at each more closely.

CONSULTANTS

Architects, architectural technologists, interior designers, and designers will all be referred to as consultants for the purposes of this section. Essentially, we are talking about people who have educational backgrounds and experience in planning and executing residential improvement projects. These are people who do not get involved with contracting the work directly, but who operate as liaisons between the contractors and the customer. The fees of these people vary accordingly, depending on their background.

Architects are perhaps the most expensive, and a true architect will be a member of a recognized architectural association. While certainly well qualified for working on residential improvements, most architects do not specialize in residential renovations. They spend a good deal of time at school, ensuring that buildings will be structurally sound, safe, and comfortable to occupy and aesthetically pleasing. Many prefer to concentrate on the aesthetics, striving for a satisfying appearance.

Because many houses are similar, and there are usually space and budget limitations, some architects do not involve themselves at all with residential work. Architectural-type services are none the less necessary for many homeowners, however, and people such as architectural technologists, designers, and others in the field help to fill this need. Many of these people are completely qualified to work in residential renovation and many, in fact, specialize in this area. Very often, the costs are somewhat less if you use this type of individual rather than an architect.

The consultant is available to provide assistance at any or all stages of the project. He or she will work on an hourly fee or, alternatively, on a percentage of the entire project. Incidentally, fees do vary and it is certainly appropriate to ask about fees before hiring anyone—even for a preliminary interview. The steps involved in completing a project are as follows and, as discussed, the consultant can help with any or all of these steps:

1. Prepare initial sketches and design drawings.
2. Prepare final working drawings and specifications.
3. Obtain building permits and variances as required.
4. Prepare tender and award contract.
5. Provide site supervision, authorize payment, and inspect as necessary.

Typically, the fees for completing step one would be 4 to 6 percent of the overall project. Payment of 10 to 12 percent of the overall project would typically include preparation of the working drawings and obtaining the permits. To follow the project through, providing supervision and inspection, the fees may range from 13 to 18 percent.

If you engage a consultant, it is important that he or she have all the information necessary to do a good job. He or she must know your budget to be able to help mesh the budget with your master plan. He or she may want to revise or refine your master plan, and he or she may rule out some of the things you have included. Do not be alarmed by this. It is part of what you are paying him or her to do. Listen carefully to his or her comments and advice, but if he or she has ruled out something that you feel particularly strongly about, do not sacrifice that component of the project. It is, after all, you who will be living with the finished product. It is often very helpful to have photographs, or illustrations from magazines, of rooms that you like, so that the consultant can get a feel for your tastes and preferences. He or she should be aware of construction materials and products available, and his or her assistance here can be invaluable.

Initial Sketches and Design Drawings

Typically, the consultant will prepare some initial sketches based on your discussions. At first, he or she may not have a fix on your tastes so this may be a period of change for both of you. Tell him or her what you want, and if you are not satisfied with his or her sketches, let him or her know.

It is also important that at this stage the major family members (usually husband and wife) both be present at meetings. It is crucial to avoid misunderstandings. Time misspent is expensive for the homeowner and frustrating for all concerned.

Working Drawings and Specifications

Once a design is prepared that appears satisfactory to all parties, the next step is to prepare the final working drawings and specifications. If it is apparent at this stage that zoning bylaw variations will have to be applied for, this can be done now to save time. At this stage you should have an approximate cost for the project, but this will have to remain flexible.

The preparation of the final working drawings and specifications will include the final cost estimate. These drawings are prepared in such a way that a contractor will be able to complete the project relying on the drawings and specifications. Sufficient detail should be provided so that the contractors do not have to make major decisions on-site. Equally important, the type and model number of components are specified. The consultant helps the owner determine such things as plumbing fixtures, door and window type, hardware quality, floor, wall, and ceiling finishes, light fixtures, etc. These components should be included in the specifications, and the contractor need only refer to these to know exactly what is to be provided. If the designer knows that some products will be difficult to obtain, or that there will be a considerable lag between order date and supply date, the process can be accelerated here.

Building Permits and Awarding the Contract

Once the drawings and specifications have been approved by the owner, application for a building permit is made. At the same time, a tender is submitted to a number of contractors for quotations. The consultant should be able to identify contractors qualified to undertake the work. Several quotations are usually solicited, with six or seven being a typical number, depending on the size of the project. The quotations are reviewed and compared by the consultant and owner, and ultimately the contract is awarded by the owner. Another advantage in using a consultant is that contractors usually prefer to deal with someone knowledgeable, and this is reflected in their quotations. They know that they won't have to explain the difference between a stud and a joist to the client.

One of the major advantages of dealing with a consultant is that you will have a complete set of drawings and specifications. As a result, you know exactly what you are going to end up with. Equally important, all the contractors will be quoting on exactly the same project and will not have to speculate about what you want. Without a complete set of drawings and specifications, it is almost impossible to compare quotations, for what the owner sees in his or her mind as the finished product will invariably be different from what each contractor sees.

Supervising the Work

After the contract is awarded and the work is to begin, the consultant will drop in from time to time to supervise the on-site work. If problems are encountered, he or she will be able to act as an arbitrator. Changes should be channeled through the consultant; additions or deletions to the project should be discussed. The consultant helps to authorize payment to the contractor at appropriate stages, and ensures that the quality of workmanship is satisfactory. The finished project is inspected at the completion date and usually, again, just before the warranty expires.

Choosing a Consultant

Obviously, a decision to employ a consultant throughout the project involves a long-term working relationship. It is completely acceptable to speak to several consultants before deciding who is most appropriate. The selection is sometimes difficult, but you can start with some of the basic sources. Friends or acquaintances who have had work done, and who have been satisfied, are a good place to start. Bear in mind, however, that just because a friend has had a satisfactory working relationship with a consultant is no guarantee that you will as well. It is also a good idea to look at your friend's project. It is possible that the type or quality of the project is unsatisfactory to you, or perhaps it is a good deal more sophisticated than you had in mind.

Associations of architects, designers, and related professionals may be able to provide names of people active in this type of work. In some cases, the junior members of large architectural firms get involved in renovations, and they, too, can be contacted. It is important to look at previous work, either by visiting the project or by looking at photographs.

Equally important is your ability to establish a good working relationship with a consultant. The more he or she knows about your preferences and lifestyle, the better he will be able to serve you.

In summary, using a consultant has several advantages. First, his or her creative ability should be an asset in any home improvement. Second, his or her knowledge and experience with residential construction, zoning bylaws, contractors, and the availability of materials should help make the work go smoothly. The preparation of drawings and specifications ensures that you know what you are getting and facilitates getting competitive quotations from the contractors. Employing a third party also simplifies things, for you are essentially dealing with one person for all of the questions, decisions, and problems you may have. Chances are good that the project will be completed near the target date.

The principal disadvantage of working with a consultant is the cost involved and the fact that, in a sense, all your eggs are in one basket. If the consultant does not meet your expectations, or cannot establish a good rapport with you, the project becomes much more difficult. Generally, the larger and more complex the project and the less experience the homeowner has, the more sense it makes to engage a professional consultant throughout.

GENERAL CONTRACTORS

A general contractor is a small businessperson who very often concerns herself with residential improvements. She is a "general" contractor in the sense that she deals with a large number of trades and is capable of providing a number of services. A general contractor may operate as a broker, hiring the appropriate subcontractors for each individual job. Alternatively, she may have some crews of the commonly used tradespeople on staff. Depending on the job, she may hire additional subcontractors as necessary.

The general contractor usually marks up the cost of the job quoted to her by the subcontractor anywhere from 10 to 50 percent. For this fee, she will obtain the subcontractors, direct their work, and take responsibility for the results.

Contractors who specialize in renovation work are in a tough, competitive business. Every job is a custom project that requires a good deal of versatility and flexibility from the tradespeople. It is often difficult to match new work to old and many surprises are hidden under old wall coverings.

Many general contractors are former tradespeople who may possess few management skills. Some do not fully understand the difference between markup and margin and, consequently, many jobs are underquoted. To end up with a 33 percent gross profit margin, a contractor must mark up her costs by 50 percent. For example, if her cost to complete a job is $1,000, and she marks it up 50 percent, the total job will be $1,500 to the customer. This leaves the contractor with a gross profit of $500 or 33 percent. A significant number of general contractors end up working essentially for wages, or going out of business altogether.

The typical general contractor can be characterized as overworked and underpaid. Her business is one that is very difficult to schedule. During the winter months there is very little activity, and during the summer months she is often deluged with work. Her manpower needs are difficult to estimate, and when she wants to hire subcontractors, many other general contractors are also trying to secure the services of good subcontractors.

The estimating procedures of most general contractors are somewhat informal. Stories about quotations on large residential projects provided on the back of cigarette packages are well known. On the other hand, it should be understood that the blame does not always rest with the general contractor. Perhaps this type of submission is appropriate, when the only drawings the contractor has to work from are those provided on a matchbook cover. In any case, the opportunity for misunderstanding and for underestimating or overestimating is tremendous.

Another problem for a general contractor is working around her client. Very often the family remains in the house during a project and this is more difficult for the workers. Tradespeople working on a project are no different from anyone else. They don't like to have another person looking over their shoulders, giving them advice or asking questions.

It is difficult to judge the performance of a general contractor as the project progresses. For many of the tasks, there is no clearly defined right or wrong way to proceed. Again, because every circumstance is different, there is very little standardization.

What are the advantages of working with a general contractor? First, she is less costly than dealing with a consultant throughout the project. The homeowner, again, only deals with one person who takes responsibility for all the subtrades' work. The general contractor also has the contacts and presumably can engage good tradespeople with whom she has some type of working relationship. The tradespeople may be more likely to do good work for the general contractor because future business is usually available from her. This is often not the case working at a one-time job for a homeowner. The general contractor is also able to plan and schedule the work so that it flows smoothly. She is able to act as a referee in any disagreement between the owner and the subcontractor. Many general contractors also offer a guarantee, which may be important should things go wrong. And if the contractor is a well-known and respected firm, it may make it easier to get a construction loan.

The disadvantages? Generally speaking, she is not a specialist in design and the preparation of drawings and specifications. While she will have experience in obtaining building permits, she may not have the background to foresee all of the problems, As discussed, it is tough to get competitive quotes from a general contractor without knowing exactly what the project is. Most of these people are not eager to do a lot of design work when preparing a quotation for a job they may not get. With a general contractor, there is often no assurance that the subcontractors are being paid, and dissatisfied subcontractors have been known to come directly to an owner asking for payment. This can create a difficult situation. General contractors do not provide impartial supervision. Their interest is in getting the job done on time and on budget, and the temptation to cut corners is obviously there.

Working with a general contractor is usually best for people who know exactly what they want from the project and have prepared working drawings and specifications, either by themselves or with the assistance of a professional. People using general contractors should either shop among several firms or should be very comfortable with the firm they engage. The owner should know enough about building construction to be able to evaluate and discuss the workmanship as the project carries on. The owner should also understand construction contracts and the liabilities and responsibilities of the various parties.

SUBCONTRACTORS

Subcontractors are individual tradespeople, usually with one special skill. Carpenters, electricians, and plumbers, among others, fit into this category. These tradespeople are available directly to homeowners or to general contractors. In many cases, subcontractors work closely with one or more general contractors. On a particular job, a subcontractor may quote the same job through two or more general contractors.

Most subcontractors work under the same hardships as general contractors do, but scheduling and organizing different trades is not a problem for them. Subcontractors rarely get involved with significant design or planning work, and usually are less involved with obtaining permits, unless they are for specialized trades. Some subcontractors operate slightly outside their field on small jobs where hiring an additional trade may not be justified. For example, many plumbers have to perform minor framing work to make the house accommodate the plumbing piping.

The advantage of dealing with a subcontractor is that the supervisory and administrative fees of the general contractor are eliminated. You also have the opportunity to select your subcontractors individually and, for people who have good contacts in the trades, this may be important. And when dealing with a subcontractor, the owner is able to ensure that payments are made appropriately and to the correct people.

The disadvantages include having to shop for a number of reliable people instead of one and being responsible for your own scheduling and arrangement of work. There is no outside supervision, and the burden lies with the homeowner. Also, arranging municipal inspections is often a job for the homeowner in this case. When problems are encountered, one subcontractor will often blame another for the failure. It is then difficult to establish responsibility, and the owner is often left less than satisfied.

Homeowners who use subcontractors typically have a good deal of experience and ability in working with and managing tradespeople. They need a good understanding of construction for they will be doing their own scheduling and supervision. A great deal of free time is required of the homeowner acting as his own general contractor. No matter how well qualified the owner is, it is typical for the subcontractor to provide less service to the owner than to a general contractor. As mentioned previously, a subcontractor is more likely to meet a deadline for a general contractor who will give him business in the immediate future than for a homeowner who, at best, may give him future referrals.

DOING IT YOURSELF

This approach can be the most rewarding or the most frustrating of all. The true do-it-yourselfer can plan, budget, design, secure building permits, order materials, and complete the work. Not only is money saved, but often the results are equal to or better than those achieved by the average tradesperson. An additional benefit is derived by those who truly enjoy doing the work; for these people a do-it-yourself project can be a recreation. Another advantage is the built-in supervisory capacity of the homeowner. The amateur often has more patience and takes more pride in his work because he knows that he will have to live with whatever mistakes are made. Also, because he is not working at an hourly rate, he may be more inclined to back up and do work again that was not completed satisfactorily the first time around. The do-it-yourselfer also has absolute control over the finances, and no disputes to arbitrate. And he is better able to shop carefully, and exhaustively, for specialized materials, such as a particular molding, old doors, or a certain ceramic tile.

There are, however, some drawbacks to being a do-it-yourselfer. Few individuals are completely skilled at all building trades. It is often not wise for the owner to attempt to learn a new skill while working on his home. It is possible that by the time he masters the trade, the work on his house will be finished and he will have made all his mistakes in the only piece of work he will ever do. What is worse, he will have to live with those mistakes. The owner should be realistic when evaluating his skills.

Different areas of work will generate different savings for the owner. While the labor costs and contractor's profits are eliminated by the do-it-yourselfer, this may or may not be a significant percentage of the total job. Doing the labor-intensive work can yield significant savings. This includes such tasks as demolition, concrete work, painting, and cleanup. For other jobs such as framing and flooring installation, material costs may represent 50 percent of the cost or more. Here, of course, the savings for the do-it-yourselfer are less. The chart provided here indicates the material-labor breakdown for a number of common trades. The contractors' markup is calculated at 50 percent, yielding a 33 percent profit margin.

Some work requires special equipment to which the amateur may not have access. Even if the equipment is available, an individual not familiar with it can get into trouble. A power sander used to take down a softwood floor is difficult to operate without damaging the floor. Scaffolding can be rented to work on high buildings, but that does not mean a person will be comfortable or safe using it.

Another consideration is time. The homeowner should be realistic in his commitment to the project. Holding a full-time job, spending time working on a project, and keeping a family together can be very difficult in a house under renovation. The enthusiasm carried through the planning process and into the first month or two of the project often wanes with a change in season, when the novelty wears off, or when the end is not in sight.

The do-it-yourselfer must allow for interruptions caused by the weather, unavailable materials, strikes, financial pressures, family emergencies, and unforeseen construction problems. Few and far between are those people who overestimate the time required to complete a project. This includes the contractors who do it for a living. The idea of a home improvement project is to make a house a better one in which to live and to increase its value. An unfinished job does neither. Contractors are not usually eager to finish work started by someone else.

Typical Renovation Costs:
Breakdown of Material versus Labor

	% Material	% Labor	% Contractor's Margin
Demolition or tear out	—	67	33
Excavation	—	67	33
Grading (topsoil added)	47	20	33
Sodding	43	24	33
Concrete work (floor slabs, footings, etc.)	32	35	33
Masonry work (brick or block)	28	39	33
Parging (with ½-inch cement, two coats)	34	33	33
Stucco wall finish (exterior)	20	47	33
Floor framing	49	18	33
Remove and replace subflooring	38	29	33
Wall framing	35	32	33
Wall sheathing	46	21	33
Roof framing	45	22	33
Roof sheathing	46	21	33
Asphalt shingle or roll roofing, cedar shingles or shakes	40	27	33

Note: Applies to simple roofs only. For dormers, valleys, two-story and three-story houses, and steep pitches, the labor percentage increases.

Downspouts	38	29	33
Exterior wood or aluminum trim	40	27	33
Wood deck	50	17	33
Wood siding	53	14	33
Aluminum siding	43	24	33
Sliding glass doors (exterior)	55	12	33
Wood doors (exterior)	50	27	33

Typical Renovation Costs:
Breakdown of Material versus Labor (Continued)

	% Material	% Labor	% Contractor's Margin
Windows	49	28	33
Plumbing (new piping and fixtures)	20-25	47-42	33
Heating (new furnace or boiler)	41-48	26-19	33
Furnace humidifier	25	42	33
Electrical work	15-20	52-47	33
Insulation	40	27	33
Drywall	26	41	33
Plywood paneling	33	34	33
Interior wood moldings and trim	37	30	33
Cabinet work	56	11	33
Carpeting	57	10	33
Painting	8-15	59-52	33

ZONING BYLAWS, BUILDING CODES, AND PERMITS

When changes are planned for a residence, local building officials are usually interested. Their concern is, first, that what you are building is structurally sound and safe; and second, that you do not create problems for your neighbors. For most renovations, you will have to submit your plans for approval to secure a building permit. Prior to issuing a permit, plans are checked for code compliance (structural integrity, safety, etc.) and for zoning bylaw compliance (protecting your neighbors).

Issuing permits for renovation work is often difficult for the authorities. Many existing structures were built before bylaws or building codes were established and, consequently, do not comply. These buildings are often referred to as *legal nonconforming*. When making changes to an existing building, it is difficult to join new conforming work and older nonconforming buildings. Although a neighbor's rights may have been slightly violated by the old structure, this does not justify worsening the situation.

Many municipalities establish special committees to which an owner can apply for a bylaw variance if she has been refused a permit. Often, the neighbors are solicited and if they have no objections, the work is approved. Variances are not usually available from building code requirements.

Zoning bylaws are different from area to area and even from lot to lot in the same municipality. Therefore, you must be careful when planning work. If a neighbor has added a sun room to his kitchen, this does not mean that you can, even if your houses and lot sizes are the same. Bylaws regulate such things as the height of the building; distances from the front, side, and back property lines; the portion of your lot that can be covered by buildings; the ratio of living area in your house to the area of the lot; parking requirements; and the number of dwelling units in a building. Because other factors may come into play, it is always best to check first with the authorities.

The building code dictates such things as foundation wall type and size, the size and span of floor and ceiling joists, material type and installation technique for interior and exterior finishes, doors, and windows. The applicable code may be a federal, provincial, state, or municipal document.

Heating, plumbing, and electrical systems can be dealt with in the building code or through a separate code.

Sometimes it is difficult to know whether a building permit is needed. Generally speaking, alterations affecting the structure will require a permit. For example, relocating a nonbearing partition wall usually does not require a permit. However, removing all or part of a bearing wall does. A permit is needed to add a window or a staircase, or to change the roof line. In some cases, a demolition permit may be necessary to remove an existing structure. If the plumbing system is to be changed, a plumbing permit may be needed. Adding a kitchen, bathroom, sauna, or laundry area will require a plumbing permit. Remodeling a bathroom may not necessitate a permit if the plumbing fixtures will be left where they are. An electrical permit is usually obtained if you are adding to the electrical service. For instance, an additional outlet or light fixture should not be installed without a permit. Replacing a defective outlet or fixture would not require a permit. Occasionally, it is necessary to move a wall with wiring inside. If the wall is moved so that the wiring is closer to the supply than it was (so that no new wire is needed), you may not need a permit. If the wall is moved away from the supply (so that you have to add a new length of wire), you will need a permit. A heating permit is usually needed if a furnace is replaced or major changes in the distribution system are undertaken.

The important point is to check with the authorities at the outset to determine what is allowed. For the most part, these people are interested in improving the community and will provide all the assistance they can.

If permits are required, allow sufficient time for them to be issued. Where you will need a variance, increase that time. It is not unusual for permits to take several weeks to be issued. Find out how much the permits cost and include these figures in your budget.

Whether or not a permit is required, you should make sure you know where your property lines are. If you have a survey of the lot, this may be all you need. If you don't have a survey, one can be made. It is almost as important that your neighbors agree on the location of the property lines. Even if your neighbor is wrong, he may be able to delay work on your project while the dispute is straightened out.

Associated with building permits are inspections. It is to your advantage to have these inspections performed, and you should assist the authorities by notifying them when the project is ready for inspection. This will help protect you and should prevent problems after the work is completed. If you are a do-it-yourselfer, inspections are equally important.

THE CONTRACT

Whenever general contractors or subcontractors are engaged, and whether or not a consultant is working with you, it is important to have a complete and clear contract. Two types of contracts are commonly employed: the fixed-price contract and the cost-plus contract.

The fixed-price contract is one with a set figure for the entire job. This allows the owner to know her costs before work starts and thus provides her with some security. Most home improvement projects are undertaken on this basis. One drawback is that the price usually includes a contingency for the contractor in case he has made any errors in his estimating. Another problem with this approach is that if the contractor has underquoted, he may be pressured to cut corners and to work out quick solutions to the unforeseen problems that always arise. He may push his crews to finish quickly, often sacrificing quality.

The cost-plus contract is one in which an hourly fee is set over and above the contractor's fixed costs. This way the contingency is not required by the contractor and the customer does not pay for it. In this circumstance, the contractor is not forced to rush his work and, theoretically, a higher-quality finished product may be enjoyed. The obvious danger, however, is that the workers may not progress at even a moderate pace, and the crews may be pulled off a cost-plus job to finish a fixed-price project more quickly. As a result, not many contracts are negotiated on this basis.

The drawings and specifications should be part of either type of contract. The specifications should be as detailed and as accurate as possible. For example, brand names, model numbers, and colors should be specified wherever possible. The type, thickness, and grade of wood should be stated. Finish materials should also be clearly identified. If you just indicate drywall, the contractor can choose ⅜-inch-, ½-inch-, or ⅝-inch-thick drywall; he can use waterproof or nonwaterproof drywall; he can glue it on, nail it on, or screw it on. It is a good idea to look at your drawings and specifications, pretending you are trying to minimize costs within the parameters of these documents. Each place you have a choice, select the least expensive material or method. Then you must decide whether the finished product will be what you want.

Where new work is to join old (brick walls, for example), colors and materials should fit together well. This may be handled with a statement such as "Items to match existing as closely as possible, and be subject to customer or consultant approval prior to installation."

There is a limit to how detailed the specifications should be. The tradespeople should not be told how to do their jobs. Overspecifying will make contractors nervous, and this is usually reflected in their quotations. A fine line must be drawn, and only with experience will you be able to determine what is appropriate. Here, again, a consultant can be very helpful.

Contracts are available in many forms and it may be useful to pick up a sample from a construction association or architect in your municipality. Or take a look at the one in this chapter. This will give you an indication of what is usually included. A number of the areas are standardized and should be common to all contracts. Some of the highlights will be presented here.

Any good contract should contain a starting and completion date for the work. Many contractors are reluctant to commit themselves to a completion date, but a target should be established. Some owners like to include a penalty clause that would come into play if the project is not completed on time. Most builders will not work on this basis, although some may agree, if there is also a bonus clause for early completion.

The payment schedule should be spelled out in the contract. If money is to be held back from each payment, this should be clearly stated. Getting off on the wrong foot because of a payment misunderstanding is unfortunate and unnecessary.

The contractor's guarantee should also be part of the contract. A means for canceling the contract by either party and a way to handle changes should be included. If a consultant is involved, his role should be explained. The contractor may be required to show proof of workers' compensation and liability insurance.

A binding contract must be signed by all the owners of the house and usually by an officer of the contracting firm. A salesperson's signature generally is not adequate. It is good practice to have your lawyer look at the contract before you sign. You should also check with your insurance agent to determine whether your house insurance will be affected and also to discuss increasing the amount of coverage. Presumably you are adding to the value of the building.

A contract often does not seem necessary at the outset when everyone is getting along well and enthusiastic about the project. And many contractors will be quite happy to work without formal documents. When problems arise, however, it is important to have a written agreement to fall back on. Good builders know that the contract also protects them from unreasonable clients.

ABC GENERAL CONTRACTING

123 4th Street
Townville, New York

CONSTRUCTION CONTRACT

Contract Date _____
Home Telephone _____
Office Telephone _____

The undersigned agrees to furnish materials, tools, equipment, and supplies and to execute in a substantial workmanlike manner according to accepted trade practices on the property described as the following work:

The following contract documents form part of this agreement:

(Working drawings and specifications listed here)

The following items are specifically excluded from this agreement and are to be furnished by others or treated as additional work:

Allowances—The following amounts are included as allowances for the items listed. In the event that costs are less than the allowance, the difference shall be credited to the Owner. In the event that costs are greater, the Contractor shall be reimbursed for the excess.

Light Fixtures and Chimes	$	Other	$
Finish Hardware	$	Other	$
Bath Accessories	$	Other	$

Finish hardware is interpreted to include all knobs, pulls, hinges, catches, locks, drawer slides, accessories, or other items that are normally installed subsequent to final painting.

Light fixtures are interpreted to include only those fixtures that are surface mounted. Bath accessories are interpreted to include medicine cabinets, towel bars, paper holders, soap dishes, etc.

PAYMENT

Subject to a holdback of ____ percent, the Owner shall:

A: Make monthly payments to the Contractor, on account, of the contract price, based on the proportion of work completed.

B: Within 15 days of the date of substantial completion, make full payment, less allowances for outstanding work and applicable holdbacks.

C: Within 15 days of the total completion and expiry of all liens, make full payment.

Contractor agrees to commence work on or about and to diligently pursue work through to completion (with extra time allowed per paragraph 16 on the reverse side hereof).

Completion to be approximately _____

Special remarks:

Because of market fluctuations in lumber and other material costs, the Contractor reserves the right to make adjustments at the time of monthly billing based on current material quotations received from suppliers.

In view of changing labor and material conditions, this contract is subject to review unless accepted in writing and this or other mutually acceptable agreement signed within 30 days of contract date.

By _____

Contractor's Licence No. _____

Salesman's Licence No. _____

Acceptance _____

Contractor is authorized to proceed with the work listed in this contract according to the terms and conditions on the reverse side hereof, which are acknowledged as part of this agreement.

Accepted _____

Accepted _____

Date _____

TERMS AND CONDITIONS

1. Extra Work

During progress of construction, the Owner may order extra work. The amount for such extra work shall be determined in advance, if possible, or may be charged for at actual cost of labor and material plus 20 percent for Contractor's overhead and fee. All sums for extras shall be due and payable upon completion of each extra.

2. Matching Material

Contractor calls attention of the Owner to the limitations of matching plaster, stucco, concrete, masonry, and roofing materials, and while Contractor shall make every effort to match existing materials, texture, colors, and planes, exact duplication is not promised. Owner to approve materials prior to installation.

3. Electrical Service

Unless specifically included, electrical work contemplates no change to existing service panel other than the addition of circuit breakers or fuse blocks to distribute electric current to new outlets. Cost incurred in changing point of service, main switch, or meter that may be required by inspector or serving utility shall be paid to the Contractor by the Owner the same as any other extra. Changes to existing wiring in areas undisturbed by alterations not included.

4. Filled Ground, Rock, or Springs

In event filled ground is encountered or rock (or any other material not removable by ordinary hand tools), Owner shall pay cost plus 20 percent of Contractor's fee. If springs are encountered, they will be dealt with at Owner's expense after discussion with Owner.

5. Property Lines

Owner shall furnish, at own expense, all surveys of property and assume all responsibility for accuracy of markers unless otherwise agreed.

6. Conduits, Pipes, Ducts

Unless specifically indicated, agreed price does not include rerouting of vents, pipes, ducts, or wiring conduits that may be discovered in removal of walls or cutting of openings in walls.

7. Access to Work Areas

Owner shall grant free access to work areas for workers and vehicles, and shall allow areas for storage of materials and rubbish. Owner agrees to keep driveways clear and available for movement and parking of trucks during normal work hours. Contractor and workers shall not be expected to keep gates closed for animals or children. Contractor shall protect adequately the property and adjacent property, subject to this contract, but shall not be responsible for damage to driveways, walks, lawns, trees, and shrubs by movement of trucks unless caused by Contractor's gross negligence.

8. Requirements of Public Bodies

Any changes, alterations, or extras from the drawings or specifications that may be required by any public body, utility, or inspector shall constitute an extra and shall be paid for the same as any other extra.

9. Materials Removed—Rubbish

All materials removed from structures in the course of alterations shall be disposed of by Contractor except those items designated by Owner prior to commencement of construction.

All construction rubbish is to be removed by Contractor at termination of work and premises left in neat broom-clean condition.

10. Insurance

Prior to commencement of construction, Owner shall have Contractor listed as loss-payee on fire and comprehensive insurance policy by means of endorsement and shall furnish waiver of subrogation for fire and those items covered under comprehensive policy including vandalism, or shall purchase separate policy to protect Contractor's interests. In event Owner fails to do so, Contractor may procure such insurance and Owner agrees to reimburse Contractor in cash for the cost thereof. Contractor shall carry at his own expense workers' compensation and public liability insurance at least to the minimum requirements of existing laws.

11. Toilet Facilities

Owner agrees to make toilet facilities available to all workers or compensate Contractor for cost of rented units.

12. Permits

Contractor shall obtain and pay for all permits required by government bodies unless otherwise specified. Owner shall secure and pay for approval of groups, or organizations, society or association, wherever such approval is required by covenant. Owner shall secure and pay for easements or other necessary property interests for permanent structures or permanent changes in existing facilities.

13. **Cancellation of Agreement**

In event of cancellation of this agreement by the Owner prior to commencement of construction, the Contractor is to receive compensation from the Owner for all expenses incurred to that date plus 5 percent of the contract price as liquidated damages and not as a penalty.

14. **Underground Pipes**

Contractor shall be not held responsible for damage to, or removing of, pipes, sprinkler lines, water, or sewage disposal systems or conduits in areas of excavation, grading, paving, or construction.

15. **Damage to Property**

Contractor shall not be held responsible for damage caused by Owner or Owner's agent or Owner's employees, act of God, soil slippage, earthquake, fire, riot, or civil commotion or acts of public enemy.

16. **Extra Time**

Contractor agrees to diligently pursue work through to completion, but shall not be responsible for delays for any of the following reasons: acts of neglect or omissions of Owner or Owner's employees or Owner's agent, acts of God, stormy or inclement weather, strikes, lockouts, boycotts, or other labor union activities, extra work ordered by Owner, acts of public enemy, riots or civil commotion, inability to secure materials through regular recognized channels, imposition of government priority or allocation of materials, failure of Owner to make payments when due, or delays caused by inspections, or changes ordered by inspectors of government bodies concerned.

17. **Licensing**

Contractor informs Owner that he is licensed under the laws and statutes of the area of jurisdiction.

18. **Protection of Owner's Property**

Owner agrees to remove or to protect any personal property, inside and out, including shrubs and flowers that cannot be protected adequately by Contractor, and Contractor shall not be held responsible for damage to or loss of said items.

19. Termination of the Contract

A: By Owner:

If the Contractor fails to execute the work properly, or otherwise fails to substantially comply with the contract requirements, the Owner may terminate the Contractor's right to continue with all or part of the work, or may terminate the contract by providing written notice thereof. The Contractor shall be entitled to payment for all work satisfactorily completed prior to termination date. The Contractor's obligation for the work completed, with respect to guarantee, etc., will remain in force after termination.

B: By Contractor:

If the Owner fails to pay the Contractor amounts due him, or otherwise fails to substantially comply with the contract requirements, the Contractor may terminate the contract by providing written notice thereof. The Contractor shall be entitled to payment for all work satisfactorily completed prior to termination date. The Contractor's obligation for the work completed, with respect to guarantee, etc., will remain in force after termination.

20. Contract

The Owner shall not sign the contract in blank and is entitled to a copy at the time he signs it.

21. Sign

Contractor is authorized to display his sign until completion of work.

22. Guarantee

Work covered by this contract, including change orders issued under this contract, is guaranteed for one year following substantial completion, provided manufactured items are covered by manufacturer's guarantee, and further provided final payment is received in full within 15 days from final billing. Contractor shall not be liable for damages resulting from the use after installation of the mechanical or plumbing equipment specified herein.

11

THE WORK BEGINS

You will have spent a great deal of
time so far talking, planning, budgeting, drawing, getting permits, and
awarding contracts, but the house still looks the same. At this stage, you
are finally ready to get things under way. If everything has been handled correctly so far, this will be a time blended with large parts of satisfaction and small parts of anguish. If you have not prepared properly,
the mix is likely to be somewhat different.

Before the workers arrive, you should have the house rules laid out.
How will the workers get into the house? Front door and through the
living room or back door? Where will their truck be parked? Is there
heavy equipment to be brought in? Where will the garbage bin be
placed? If they are excavating, where will the earth be dumped? It may
not be easy protecting your landscaping or getting your car out of the
garage. These things have to be established before any damage is done.

Will you make a washroom available to the workers? If so, your guest
towels may not be appropriate. Is there a good place for the tradespeople to eat their lunch? It will help if you make waste disposal easy for
them. It is a nice gesture to offer coffee and doughnuts, but be careful
not to get too friendly with the workers. They are, after all, working for
you and you should maintain a businesslike relationship.

You should know who will be in charge of the project, and an area in the house there should be designated as your communication depot. All your questions and comments should be directed to the person in charge through this command post. If you are working with a consultant, he will usually be the liaison.

Difficult as it may be to accept, the general contractor does not usually oversee your project eight hours a day. You may not see him regularly, and a written message left at the communication post will be the best way to get in touch.

Insist on a daily cleanup program. The first day will set the tone of the project, so be firm just once and you should be in good shape throughout. If the workers are doing something incorrectly, or if you have a question, resist the temptation to speak directly to the tradesperson. Remember, all your communications should be through one person. If a major mistake is clearly being made, such as knocking down the wrong wall or putting a window in the wrong room, however, by all means stop the work and call for help.

SUPERVISION

Even if a consultant is providing site supervision, you should visit the job regularly, daily if possible. It is your house and if things are not the way you want them, now is the time to change them. You will also have a better idea of how things are put together and where they are located when the job is finished. This may stand you in good stead later with maintenance problems or future improvements. Incidentally, as things begin to take shape, everything will look smaller than it did on paper. Don't panic, this impression is usually reversed by the time furnishings are in place.

Make sure the municipal inspections are made at the appropriate times. Contractors do not like to wait for inspectors, and if the work goes on without inspections, contractors are not usually concerned. Inspectors will not ordinarily demand that walls be opened up to inspect what they cannot see. However, good management and timing keeps life simpler for everyone.

SEQUENCE OF OPERATIONS

A renovation project, large or small, is a complex operation, and a proper sequence must be followed to produce a smooth flow. We will look briefly at the steps involved and try to decide why they must be done in this order.

First, we must look outside. If the job is anything less than a total gutting of the house, it is important that the building be kept weather-proof. It is an absolute crime to have your newly finished bedroom ceiling ruined by a tiny roof leak. If the house is to be gutted and redone, the roof is usually left as is until all the vents and chimneys penetrate it, then the roof is resurfaced before the interior finishes are applied.

The demolition work comes next: removing wall and ceiling finishes, tearing down walls and pulling apart kitchens and bathrooms. This will be your first opportunity to see what order the contractor can maintain and how well he cleans up the site.

The structural work is next. New walls, floors, doorways, stairs, and openings are created. This is the skeletal work. The initial building inspection is conducted at this stage.

Heating comes next with ductwork or piping tucked in between the stud spaces and floor joists. Plumbing is roughed in next with the piping placed between the framing members and the heating distribution ductwork. Fixtures are not usually in place at this point, with the possible exception of the bathtub. Electrical work follows with the wiring installed for present and future uses. Wires are left unfinished at their termination points until wall and ceiling finishes are applied.

The reason heating, plumbing, and wiring are dealt with in that order is that the wiring is more flexible than the plumbing, which, in turn, is more flexible than the heating. These systems are now ready for the initial inspection.

The new windows and doors can be added at this point. Insulation can be fitted in as well. Plumbing, heating, and electrical people understandably try to avoid working in insulated walls.

We are now ready for the interior wall and ceiling finishes to be added. As long as the exterior is protected from the weather, outdoor work can be completed at any time, weather permitting.

Finish carpentry and cabinetwork, as well as wood trim, are added next. Kitchen cupboards, tile work, closets, and countertops are finished at this point.

The plumbers, heating contractors, and electricians come back to complete their systems. Fixtures are installed and tested, and final inspection of the work of these tradespeople is conducted.

Decorating is undertaken, with floor finishes added, door hardware installed, and the last touches applied. This brings the project to an end and everything should be perfect.

At this stage, disappointment can set in. While you are scrutinizing the work, flaws leap out at you. There are a hundred things that are not right or that could have been done slightly better. You have paid a lot of money, why didn't the workers take just a little more time? This is a good time to go for a walk through a new subdivision. Chances are you will find houses there are not perfect either. It begins to become apparent that your job will not be quite as good as it looked on paper. But understanding that no renovation project is flawless should help console you.

You can negotiate with your contractor, and with the help of a consultant agree on what flaws are to be corrected. Certain things are clearcut, but others, which are a question of workmanship, are difficult to identify specifically as defects. You will probably have to trade off on some of your improvement and repair expectations. Keep in mind, however, that no one will ever look at your house as closely as you are looking at it now. Once you move your furniture in, it will not be exposed to such close examination.

In short, prepare yourself for something less than 100 percent. Aim for perfection by all means, but be realistic in your expectations. For you, every piece of work in the house is exciting and important; however, for the tradespeople, it is just another day at work and they, after all, will not be living in the house.

One last thing before you say good-bye to the contractor. Make sure that you have all the warranties or guarantees for new appliances or fixtures. The contractor will have no use for them and you should keep them on file. You will also want to keep a set of working drawings and specifications on file. Make sure you get a set.

PAYING FOR THE WORK

One of the most common mistakes made by homeowners during a renovation project is to pay too much money up front. The payment is the only trump card you hold, and it is the best way to ensure that the game is played properly and completely. If you have paid in advance, and difficulties arise, you will find yourself negotiating from a position of weakness rather than strength.

Large Projects

Large projects are expected to take several months. Many contractors will ask for a large down payment before work is started and will tell you that this is how they do business. Be very careful at this point. Unless materials are unusually expensive or have to be ordered well in advance, with a large deposit, you should not put down a large percentage of the money. Many contractors do not pay cash for their supplies and should not be heavily burdened by getting materials to the job. Typically, a 10 percent down payment would be maximum. Also ensure that an appropriate receipt is received. The contract should spell out the payment schedule.

The next payment should be made after materials are on-site and the first stages of the work have been satisfactorily completed. If the work is not right, do not make a payment. Each payment should represent an appropriate proportion of the project, less a predetermined holdback. The holdback is for mechanics' liens that will be discussed shortly.

The payment calculation works this way. For instance, after two weeks, 20 percent of the work is completed to your satisfaction. If the contract amount is $10,000, the payment is $2,000 less 10 percent (typical) holdback. The payment then is $1,800 ($2,000 × 90% =). This approach is carried through the project. For example, when the project is 80 percent complete, you will have paid $7,200 ($10,000 × 80% × 90%). At the completion of the work, you will have paid $9,000, the full $10,000 contract amount less the 10 percent holdback. This amount is typically withheld for approximately 40 days to protect against mechanics' liens.

A lien is a claim against your property by someone who has supplied materials or performed work in it. The question of liens is a somewhat confusing and complicated issue, and in many areas there is no complete agreement on its meaning. The concept arose as a method of providing suppliers and subcontractors with some protection when they supplied materials or did work on a house. For example, an owner engages a general contractor, who, in turn, hires a subcontractor. The subcontractor does the work, the owner pays the general contractor, but the general contractor doesn't pay the subcontractor. The subcontractor is in a difficult position. He has put his materials and labor into the house, but has no contractual relationship with the owner.

If the general contractor is uncooperative, or cannot be located, the situation is unsatisfactory for everyone. Thus, it was decided that if someone provided work or materials, he could stake a claim on the subject property if he was not paid. Although the time may vary in different areas, the supplier or subcontractor typically has 40 days after completing his work to register a lien. A house with a lien outstanding is very difficult to sell. As a result of this protection for the subtrades, the owner can be put in a delicate position. He may pay the general contractor in good faith only to discover that the general contractor has failed to pay the subcontractor. Contracts between general contractors and subcontractors are often loose or nonexistent. If the subcontractor puts a lien on the property, he has a legal claim to part of the value of the house. Even though you have paid for the work!

A partial solution is to hold back approximately 10 percent from each payment. It is important that you do not make payments in full up to the point where 90 percent of the work is complete, then withhold the balance. This protects neither you nor the subcontractor. For example, the first subcontractor who worked on the project may have been the contractor who poured the concrete. His work may have been completed within the first two or three days of the project. If the general contractor is paid in full for this work and the subcontractor puts a lien on the property, the owner has nothing left from the funds allocated to this part of the project. If the general contractor abandons the project with 90 percent payment and 90 percent of the work completed, the owner has no protection against liens. Another problem is that by not holding back 10 percent from the first payment, the owner may forfeit his right to hold back anything from future payments.

The 10 percent holdback figure is somewhat arbitrary and may or may not be enough to pay off a subcontractor. It could just as easily be established at 20 percent. This is now a tool used to protect an owner, even though it was designed originally to protect the subcontractor.

Before making the final payment of 10 percent, verify that the time limit for subcontractors to register a lien has expired and that there are, in fact, no liens against the property. One final word about holdbacks. Many experts recommend that holdbacks toward the end of the project should be proportionately greater than those made earlier. For some reason, it is common for owners to have difficulty getting the last of the work finished. If another contractor is brought in to complete the job, it is likely to be expensive. Remember, the only motivator the owner has is the money he has not paid. One of the reasons a lawyer should look at the contract is that he will be able to advise on holdbacks and lien requirements. Interpretations and procedures may vary from place to place and it is best to get professional advice at the outset.

The completion date of the project itself is often difficult to determine. Most contracts refer to a "substantial completion date." This is the date that starts the clock on the 40 days the subcontractors have to place their liens. It is also the beginning of the contractor's guarantee period (usually one year). This is defined as the day on which work is substantially complete. This sounds like a poor definition, and it is. In practice, this date is considered the one on which all work is finished except for minor touch-up or repair. The renovation should be habitable and the only outstanding work of consequence should be the result of forces beyond the control of the contractor. For example, if the owner has changed his mind about the light fixtures he wants and the new fixtures are not immediately available, the contractor is not at fault. If, however, the originally specified bathroom faucets are imported and take two months to arrive but the contractor didn't order them until two weeks before they were needed, the contract is probably not substantially completed until they arrive and are installed.

It is usually to the contractor's advantage to declare the substantial completion date as early as he can so that he can be paid as soon as possible. The owner may try to delay the date to postpone his payments. Again, a consultant can be of assistance here.

If difficulties are experienced in getting the work finished, the owner can notify the contractor that he is soliciting quotations from other contractors to complete the work. He advises the contractor that unless action is taken by a given date, a new contract will be awarded. The cancellation clause in the original contract should, of course, be referred to.

Smaller Projects

Renovations that are expected to take days to weeks to complete require a different approach. The bulk of the materials required to complete the project are often ordered and delivered immediately. As a result, payment is usually made in larger chunks. A 30 percent down payment may be expected, with another 30 percent to be paid while work is in progress. A final 30 percent should be paid when the work is substantially complete, while 10 percent should be kept as a holdback. The second 30 percent may be paid when the work is one-half to two-thirds complete, or when the subtradespeople need their first or second payment. Whatever is decided, make sure that the contract clearly spells out the timing of payments.

SUMMARY

A renovation is a complex undertaking. The potential for problems is tremendous, and even with all the correct steps taken, things can and do go wrong. The renovation business is a difficult one, and both the contractors and owners need all the protection they can get. The larger the job and the less knowledgeable the owner, the more outside help he will need.

The most important thing is to be honest with yourself. Look realistically at your budget, your knowledge of construction, your skills, and your time. If you can take advantage of your strengths and get help with your weaknesses, the chances of success are good. Keep in mind that this should be an enjoyable experience, before, during, and after the actual work.

ampere (amp) A unit defining the rate of flow of electricity (a unit of current).

beam A horizontal structural component, usually wood or steel, that is typically supported by a foundation wall or column. A beam is generally used to support floor joists.

blower A device shaped like a squirrel cage and found in a furnace or air-conditioning unit. It serves as a fan to blow conditioned air through the ductwork of a house.

caulk To fill seams and joints with a flexible durable substance (caulking) to make them watertight and to reduce air leakage.

circuit breaker An automatic switch used in a panel box that disconnects the flow of electrical current whenever the circuit is overloaded. The breaker may be reset when the problem is solved.

collar ties Horizontal framing members in an attic used to tie roof rafters together and stiffen the roof.

column A pillar or post usually supporting a beam.

compressor The component of an air-conditioning or heat-pump system that forces refrigerant to travel through the system and also changes a low-pressure vapor to a high-pressure vapor. It is usually located outdoors.

concrete The finished or hardened product after cement, sand, gravel, and water are mixed.

condensate The water that drips from a cooling coil on an air-conditioning system and flows to a drain.

condenser The portion of an air-conditioning system that cools hot refrigerant vapor to the point where it becomes a liquid. It is usually located outdoors.

course On a roof, this is a continuous or level row of shingles. In a masonry wall, it is a row of bricks or stones.

efflorescence A white powdery substance that appears on masonry wall surfaces. It is composed of soluble salts that have been brought to the wall surface by water seepage.

evaporator The portion of an air-conditioning system installed in the ductwork above a furnace. Its function is to cause liquid to expand suddenly into a gas, thus causing an evaporation and cooling effect. Heat is drawn from the air passing over the evaporator.

fascia A board that is nailed vertically to the lower ends of roof rafters. Visible from the building exterior, it is sometimes used to support the gutters.

flashing Sheet metal or other material used around chimneys, projecting pipes, or in roof valleys to prevent water from entering at joints.

flue An enclosed passageway within a chimney for carrying off smoke and gases.

footing An enlargement at the bottom of a wall or column for the purpose of spreading the weight over a larger area. It is usually made of concrete.

fuse An electrical device that interrupts the flow of electrical current when the circuit is overloaded. Unlike a circuit breaker, a fuse must be replaced once it has blown.

gable The vertical triangular section of a wall formed by two converging roof lines.

grade The ground level around a building.

gutter The trough at the bottom of the roof that collects rainwater. Also known as an eaves trough.

heat exchanger A device by which heat is exchanged from one heat-carrying medium to another without contact between the two media.

jamb An upright piece of wood forming the side of a door or window opening.

joists Parallel boards placed on edge and used to support floor and ceiling loads. Typically, they are two-by-eights or two-by-tens.

knee wall A wall that acts as a brace by supporting roof rafters at an intermediate position along their length.

lath A backing for plaster walls that is fastened to the frame of a building. Lath is typically made of wood, metal, or gypsum board.

masonry Building materials such as brick, concrete blocks, structural clay tiles, and stone. In some areas, cement, stucco, and plaster are also classified as masonry.

nail popping A flaw common to drywall finishes. The nail head protrudes through the surface of the drywall as a result of wood shrinkage.

parging A coat of cement applied to a masonry wall. It helps to prevent foundation walls from leaking.

pointing (also known as repointing or tuckpointing) The filling of open mortar joints. Removal and replacement of deteriorated mortar from between masonry joints.

ponding The accumulation of rainwater in a depression on a flat roof.

R-value A designation for insulation, denoting its resistance to the transfer of heat. The higher the R-value, the better the insulation.

rafters A series of structural roof members, made of wood, which support the roof. Typically, these are two-by-fours or two-by-sixes.

sheathing A covering, usually wooden boards or plywood, fastened over a building's exterior studs or rafters.

soffit The visible underside of a roof overhang or eave.

square One hundred square feet of applied roofing material.

studs Wood or metal vertical structural members forming walls and partitions, normally two-by-fours or two-by-sixes.

subfloor Boards or plywood laid on joists. The finished floor is laid over this.

valley The angle formed by the meeting of two sides of a sloped roof.

vapor barrier A waterproof material placed on the warm side of insulation to prevent moisture from migrating into the insulation.

vent stack A vertical vent pipe protruding through the roof to carry away sewer gases from the plumbing system, and to prevent siphoning of traps by drawing air into the waste system.

volt A measure of electrical pressure or potential.

watt A measure of electrical power (amperes × volts = watts).

sequence of operations, 209–10
subcontractors, 192–93
supervision of, 208
zoning/codes, 196–98
Repointing, 25
Retaining walls, 6
Rigid board insulation, 157. *See also*
Insulation
Roofs/roofing, 9–19
asphalt shingles, *12,* 12–13
built-up, *16,* 16–17
checklist, 37
fiber cement shingles, 15
flat roofs, 17, 18, 173
garage, 6
ice dams, *11*
modified bitumen, 18
moisture problems, 173–74
pitch, 10, 13, 14, 15
renovation and, 209
reroofing, 13, 19
roof framing, 175–76
selvage or roll roofing, 16
slates, 13–14
slopes, *10*
specialty materials for, 18
tar and gravel, 16–17
wood shingles and shakes,
14–15, *15*
Rot, 5, 6, 176
R-value
insulation, 156, *157*
windows, 134–35

S

Saddles, 8
Safety considerations
attached garages, 6
electrical service and, 49, 60, 61,
67
exhaust fans and, 173
insulation and, 164
wood shingles, 14
Salt deposits, 108
Sandblasting, 26
Security issues, 36
Selvage/roll roofing, 16
Septic systems, 80–82, *81, 82*

Sewers, 79–80
Sheathing, 23–24
Sheds, 6–8
Shingles
asphalt, *12,* 12–13
fiber cement, 15
wood, 14–15, *15*
Sidewalks, 5
Siding
aluminum and steel, *32,* 32
insulbrick, 31
moisture damage and, 24–25
sheet, 33
vinyl, *32,* 33
wood, 31
Skylights, 136, 151
Slates, 13–14
Soffit vents, 172, 173
Soil absorption fields, 80
Soils, drainage and, 5
Spalling, 25, 26
Spanish tile, 18
Splash block, 19
Stairwells/stairways, 143, *144,*
151–52
basement, 114, 121
handrails and guards, 143, 144
lighting, *64,* 65
Storage pressure tank, 70, *71*
Storm windows, 33–34, 134–35
Structure, exterior, 39–44
analyzing crack size, *44*
checklist, 48
exterior walls, 41–43
footings, 39–40
foundation walls, 40–41
inspection, 43–44
overview of, *40*
settlement, *41*
Structure, interior, 44–47
checklist, 48
cracked joists, *45*
rot, 46
termites, 46–47
Stucco, 27–29
Studs, 42
Subcontractors, 192–93
Subflooring, *128*
Substantial completion date, 213